NEVER TRUST A SMILING BEAR

True Tales to make you Laugh, Chortle, Snicker and Feel Inspired

Edited by Matt Jackson

Summit Studios

Library and Archives Canada Cataloguing in Publication

Never trust a smiling bear : true tales to make you laugh, chortle, snicker and feel inspired / edited by Matt Jackson.

ISBN 978-0-9734671-8-5
        1. Outdoor life–Canada--Humor. 2. Voyages and travels–Humor. 3. Canadian wit and humor (English). I. Jackson, Matt

PN6178.C3N48 2010   796.50971   C2010-903148-2

Designed by Kirk Seton, Signet Design Inc.
Cover Photo by Pat Toth-Smith
Printed and bound in Canada

SUMMIT STUDIOS
#105, 2572 Birch St.
Vancouver, British Columbia
V6H 2T4 Canada

This book is dedicated to all travelers who venture forth bravely and come home with stories to share

Table of Contents

Introduction

By Matt Jackson

It's amazing the people you meet at book signings. The primary reason for these "meet and greet" events is to sell books, of course, but oftentimes they also turn into impromptu storytelling forums.

You see, people who chuckle when they first notice a title like *Mugged by a Moose* (the first in our travel and outdoor humor series) are the same kinds of people who often have amusing anecdotes to share themselves. I have heard a lot of great stories while sitting in bookstores trying to sell my wares, and every now and then I'm even able to convince one of these people to write something up and send it in for publication. Mary Wellwood is one such like-minded person.

A charming lady, Mary retired from teaching several years ago, but quickly found that retirement was just not action-packed enough for her. As a result, she applied for a teaching position on a small Ojibwa First Nations reserve in northern Manitoba, where she spent the greater part of the next five years. I met her at a book signing in London, Ontario in 2008, and when she saw the types of books that I write and edit, she couldn't help but share a personal experience with me: an ode to human-wildlife encounters that she has graciously recounted in her story "Strange

Bedfellows." It is one of my favorite stories in this collection for its sheer improbability.

Which leads me to a question that many people ask: "Where the heck do you find all these stories?" A small number come from people like Mary, of course, but the majority of them—at least the ones in this book—were collected from a travel writing contest that we ran from December 2009 until the end of January 2010. It was the second such contest that we've organized, and this time we received almost three hundred entries. This is seven times the number of entries we received during our 2004 contest.

With that many stories submitted, it's no surprise that the quality of prose in this volume is extremely high. From the subtle charm of Sarah Lolley's encounter with a cheeky monkey at a Vietnam zoo ("Monkey Business") to Don Wilkinson's testosterone-fueled off-road adventures in the Yukon wilderness ("Toyotas Don't Float"), this might very well be the best collection of travel stories we've ever assembled. And don't miss Doug Underhill's unbelievable tale of a fishing day gone *very* wrong— and then unexpectedly righting itself. His anecdote—titled simply "A Fish Story"—is the sort of scenario not even a fiction writer could have invented lest it be considered too far-fetched.

There are even a couple of award-winning travel writers in this collection. Torontonian Steve Pitt shares two laugh-out-loud yarns with us, my favorite of which is "Northwest Passage." In this he tells the tale of trying to avoid an end-of-long-weekend traffic jam while heading south on Highway 400, a situation that many residents of southern Ontario will no doubt relate to.

Then there is Robert Earle Howells, a California writer who describes a malnourished week of trekking in the Amazon Basin in "Bob of the Jungle." Among other things, he learns to eat finger-sized grubs … and enjoy them!

Pitt and Howells were two of six writers who won prizes in our most recent story contest. Stuart Reininger ("Pidge rules the Roost"), Greg Simison ("Masters of Mayhem") and Neil McKinnon ("Pains, Trains and Wildfires") were the other three secondary prizewinners.

Which brings me to our Grand Prize-winning story, "Antler Girls," penned by Sunderland, Ontario writer Lois Gordon. I must admit that when I first read Gordon's story I only hesitantly put it on my pile of possible prizewinners. Not because the story wasn't well written or laugh-out-loud funny (it's both!), but more because it was about a rather "non-adventurous" Christmas road trip to Myrtle Beach. Personally, I'm not drawn to vacation hubs like Myrtle Beach, and such a tale just didn't jive with what I had initially envisioned as a Grand Prize-winning story. On the surface, it hardly compared to Howell's extreme, grub-eating jungle escapades, or with the barely believable events that Underhill relates in his fish story.

In the end, I just couldn't ignore the craftsmanship that Gordon uses to tell her tale. Like many good travel stories, this one has an unforgettable sidekick in her friend Donna; but unlike many writers, Gordon has the uncanny knack of poking fun at her friend's quirks without rubbing readers the wrong way. This is a very difficult balance to achieve, but Gordon more than proves herself up to the challenge.

I think that's enough of a preview. Best to let our writers tell their own tales, in their own words. Just remember that there is no better tonic for travel misadventure than laughter. It's a motto worth taking to heart—especially if you find yourself in the Amazon with Jungle Bob and nothing to eat but grubs!

Pidge Rules the Roost

Who does this boat belong to anyway?

Stuart Reininger

I huddled behind the canopy as the good ship *Taurus* hurtled through the starless night. Rain rattled against the not-so-protective canvas. A trickle found its way past my slicker and down my back. I was tired, wet and cold.

I glanced at my watch: 3:00 a.m. Another hour until my daughter Karin would relieve me so that I could snatch a few moments of sleep.

We had ploughed into stiff seas driven by a nasty headwind since leaving New York five days earlier. *Taurus*, a fat luxury sloop designed for sheltered waters, rolled sickeningly when broadside to the seas and pounded with a bone-shuddering jar when running into the waves. We could expect another ten days of abuse before making St. Thomas in the U.S. Virgin Islands, where I would hand the beast over to the charter company that had hired us.

Unfortunately, believing an optimistic weather report, I had given in to the entreaties of my fourteen-year-old daughter and allowed her to accompany me. Worse yet, my partner had broken his arm two days before we were to leave, leaving only me and Karin—for whom this was supposed to be a watch-and-learn experience—to sail the boat. She, of course, saw opportunity where I only saw risk. Although she had been bought up on sailboats and was an accomplished sailor in her own right, Karin's offshore experience consisted of coastal cruising and a few overnighters— more than enough, as far as she was concerned, for her to demand full crew status.

Battling to keep my eyes open, I heard a soft fluttering over the patter of rain, followed by a muted thump. I turned around, and there, looking just as confused about being where he was as I was to see him, was a dirty, bedraggled gray pigeon: a genuine New York street bird.

"Well, hello, Pidge. How'd you get way out here?" I reached my hand out in greeting.

"Brrrrck." *Snap!*

"Ouch!" I quickly withdrew my hand, now oozing blood from a beak-tip-sized hole. "Ungrateful wretch." I glared at him.

The bird glared back. Then, clucking under his breath, he tucked his beak under a wing while keeping a beady eye focused on me.

"Wow! Look at the pigeon!" Karin exclaimed when she emerged from the cabin. The bird was hunkered on the aft deck with his head still tucked under a wing. He seemed to be fast asleep.

"Watch out," I warned, showing her my pecked hand. "He's armed and dangerous."

Karin took the helm but kept glancing aft. I knew my kid; she had a soft spot for anything vaguely cuddly. Well, I had warned her. Let her suffer the consequences.

After satisfying myself that Karin was holding the boat on course, I went below and drifted into a fitful sleep. I awoke at sunrise to find *Taurus* slicing through calmer seas. Karin looked confident at the helm. I glanced at the compass—right on course. The aft deck was deserted. Our unwelcome guest had departed, but not before leaving a mess where he had perched.

"Have a nice nap, Dad?" Karin asked. With her wide grin and damp blonde hair plastered to her forehead, she looked even younger than her fourteen years. I knew she was fishing for a compliment. She had done a good job handling the boat. But if I let her know that, she would hassle me for more responsibility.

"Yeah," I said, gesturing aft. "Glad we got rid of that nuisance. I'll clean the mess up. Go on below and get some sleep."

Karin moved from behind the helm, then turned, carefully lifted the pigeon from the seat beside her, and tucked the bird under her arm. His beady eyes looked around like he owned the place. I was astounded.

"How did you do that?"

"He's friendly," Karin gushed. "He came right over to me. You guys just got off on the wrong wing. C'mon and make up with Pidge."

I edged toward them carefully, hand tentatively outstretched.

"Brrrrck!" *Snap!*

"Ouch!"

That set the tone for my relationship with Pidge—an armed truce with mutual hostility. After it became obvious that the bird was not going to leave, Karin begged me to let him roost in the closet where we hung our foul-weather gear whenever she wasn't on watch. I reluctantly agreed, but while her relationship with Pidge blossomed, ours wilted. As both a captain and a parent I retreated into a bunker of gruff authority.

On our seventh day out, I woke from an uncomfortable catnap on deck. The seas were building, and lowering clouds indicated we were headed for nasty weather. Suspecting a long stay at the helm, I went below to get my new set of Helly Hansen foul-weather gear. I pulled my gear out and … yuck! They were splotched with a gooey yellow-green mess.

"My Hellys!" I hollered. "Look what that bird's done to my Hellys." Furious, I rushed on deck and grabbed Pidge from his usual position reposing peacefully alongside Karin.

"Dad!" Karin yelled in alarm.

"This bird has got to go!" I cried. "I've had it!"

In a rage, I tossed the pigeon overboard. I expected him to fly—probably right back to Karin. But he didn't. Screeching, he fluttered into the water and disappeared in our wake.

"Why did you do that?" Karin cried, her voice growing hysterical. "You killed him!"

"I'm sorry," I mumbled. "I thought he would fly. I don't know why he didn't. He's a bird, for Pete's sake."

"We have to go back and get him!"

"That's ridiculous." I began to explain that even if we were able to reverse course quickly, it would be hours before we could return to Pidge's exact position, and that it would be impossible to find him. There was no response, but Karin's expression forewarned a life of woe for me if I didn't at least make a valiant effort.

A sailboat going downwind is far different than one motoring into howling winds and growing seas—which was exactly our situation after I turned the boat around. For two hours we endured a cacophony of sound and motion that overwhelmed our senses. *Taurus* gyrated and bucked, groaning and shuddering each time she nosed into the building sea. Between the wind-driven rain slashing horizontally across the boat and the falling darkness, our horizon was reduced to just a few feet of storm-tossed ocean on either side of the boat. We had to get turned around and resume our downwind course before something broke.

I turned to Karin, who continued to stare resolutely ahead.

"It's no use, sweetheart," I yelled over the wind. "He's gone. We have to get going."

"Just a few minutes more," she pleaded, her face reddened by spray and tears.

After five more minutes of futile slogging, I eased the boat back on course and prepared to shut the engine and raise sail. Karin's face was etched with agony. She avoided looking at me. I turned away, my eyes also blurred.

And there, just a few yards off our port bow, was Pidge.

Pidge must have spotted us at the same time we saw him. He propelled himself towards the boat, one wing beating the water like a malfunctioning eggbeater, the other flopping uselessly at his side.

We both hollered in glee when we saw the bird. Then, just a few feet from *Taurus*, Pidge gave out. One moment he was alive; the next, he was a limp gray rag in the water, lifelessly riding the waves.

I felt sadness mixed with relief. It would have been an effort to get him aboard anyway.

"I'm sorry, honey. He's gone."

Her voice rose. "We have to get him!"

"There's no way. I can't leave the wheel."

"I'll take the wheel!" she screamed, the wind whipping her words away. "You use the wash bucket to scoop him up."

But that meant Karin would have to handle the boat while I went after the bird. It would be a dangerous maneuver. If I fell overboard there was no way she would be able to retrieve me. It wasn't worth the risk. The bird was dead.

I started to explain, but there it was again—the do-or-die look. I had to give it a shot or I might as well join Pidge in bird heaven.

Balancing on the foredeck, I pondered the near impossibility of grabbing the bird. The drop from *Taurus's* deck to the water was a good five feet and I'm a short guy; there was no way I could reach down and just grab him.

I tied a line to the bucket and heaved it overboard—useless. I looked aft and sadly gestured that I had done my best, indicating that we had to get going. Answer: a stony look.

Resignedly, I lashed the end of the bucket line to a stanchion, lay facedown on the deck, hooked my foot onto a stanchion support and, with the bucket in my hand, stretched down as far as I could reach. There he was. One more stretch…

I heard the engine kicking in and out of gear as Karin tried to hold position. *Taurus* bucked as waves slammed the hull and washed over me. I slipped and dangled over the side, my only connection to the boat my rapidly numbing ankle jammed into the stanchion support.

Suddenly my head was under water, looking at the underside of the bird. I scooped and he was in the bucket. But I realized that I might very well die while trying to climb back aboard. I envisioned the obit: *"Lost at sea trying to save a dead bird."* Then the bucket was being hauled up and I felt a line lash around my ankle. I looked up just before the plunging boat dunked my head under again. There was Karin, scowling down at me.

"Get back up here!" she screamed, then disappeared as *Taurus* began to slough sideways.

I contorted around and struggled up, finally managing to hoist myself onto the deck. I staggered aft, where Karin was trying to steer the boat and fondle Pidge at the same time. I could see that she finally realized the bird was dead; I hoped she realized that she had almost driven her dad to the same fate.

Over the years we had buried two goldfish, a canary, and a dog. As soon as we got back on course, we'd hold a little ceremony and send Pidge on his final journey.

I grabbed the helm as Karin, tears running down her face, picked the bird out of the bucket. I reached over to show a sympathy that was far from heartfelt.

"Brrrrck." *Snap!*

"Ouch!"

Pidge drew blood and glared at me with renewed malevolence. Karin let out a joyful shriek. I made a conscious effort not to grab him from her loving arms and give his neck a good twist before tossing him overboard again. Instead, I managed a weak, "How wonderful."

Karin got her bird back, and also achieved full crew status. With the two of them on deck, I deserved as much sleep as I could get.

Eight days later we made landfall. As soon as Pidge spotted St. Thomas, he emitted a loud squawk, launched himself, and— leaving a final deposit on the helm seat—disappeared toward land, propelled by a pair of powerful and obviously healthy wings.

Karin continues to crew with me. We take a cat with us now.

Still confused as to whether he's a journalist who sails or a professional mariner who writes, Stuart Reininger lives aboard his classic yacht Tall Tales when he isn't battling unwanted avian visitors from offshore.

Northwest Passage

When a shortcut turns into a lot more...

By Steve Pitt

It's early Monday afternoon on the first holiday weekend of the summer, and my son and I are stranded in our car about ten kilometers north of Barrie, Ontario. There are 113 solid kilometers of car bumpers in front of us. Highway 11 south from Gravenhurst has been stop-and-go since noon, and according to radio reports, it's about to get worse from Barrie to Toronto because multiple traffic accidents have reduced southbound traffic from four lanes to one.

I spot a clear westbound off-ramp marked "Sideroad 8" and a light comes on in my head.

In theory, all we have to do is drive about forty klicks west to bypass the north end of Barrie. From there, we should be able to cruise down Highway 27 all the way to Toronto. I ask my son if he's feeling adventurous.

He doesn't even look up from his Game Boy. "Whatever," he says.

I crank the steering wheel right and hit the gas. After ninety minutes of gridlock, the sudden rush of open road under our wheels is intoxicating. It feels so good that for the first two minutes I actually don't care that I don't have a clue where we're going—until I glance in the mirror and notice that we're being followed.

In hot pursuit of our Honda are two cars, two SUVs, a minibus, and a camper truck with a boat trailer. All of them are loaded with people suffering from the deluded notion that I know the secret Northwest Passage around Barrie to Toronto.

Now, I do have a pretty good sense of direction, but the secondary highways of Ontario follow the contours of the land, not the compass. They can change direction or even end with no warning whatsoever. In the past, many of my "shortcuts" have ended up with the road petering out to a single lane until we finally come to a dead end in front of a log cabin with a barefoot guy playing a banjo on the porch.

As long as I'm wasting my own time, I don't mind. But I don't relish having to explain this to the six carloads of strangers who are now following me faithfully through the wilderness.

I step on the gas, hoping to lose them on some tight corners. But they not only keep up, they actually manage to close the distance until we form a single rushing line of crazed kamikazes.

When Sideroad 8 suddenly veers north and looks as if it's going to keep going that way, I hang a left on Concession Road 15, which takes us southwest again for about ten kilometers. We come to a T-junction. My first instinct is to turn right, which would take us northwest. But I go left, hoping to discourage my entourage.

No such luck. One by one, they follow me like loyal ducklings, even though I see several of the drivers look longingly at the beckoning northern road.

I know that if I continue on my new route, I will soon hit the freeway again. This is definitely not what I want. Within minutes, I actually see the stalled cars on the freeway dead ahead. Then a small road called Ski Trail—bearing south—comes up fast on the right. Without signaling or even slowing, I turn.

Directly behind us is a brand new grape-green Lexus SUV. The driver is a woman in her early thirties. Even in weekend clothes, she looks as if she is wearing a power suit. (Who wears T-shirts with padded shoulders?)

She hasn't stopped talking on a cell phone since we left Highway 11. Without blinking, she throws the Lexus into a one-handed skid, recovers, and lands back on course. In fact, she hasn't blinked since we left the highway.

Vehicle number two is a maroon Volvo station wagon with mountain bikes lashed to the roof; through the windshield, I see the silhouettes of several children clinging to their mother like baby possums. Aided by antilock brakes and power steering, the Volvo easily makes the turn, but one of the bikes on the roof is now tilting at a forty-five-degree angle.

One by one, the other vehicles follow. A black Ford Explorer crammed full of kids and huge drooling dogs is right behind the Volvo. After a grinding right turn, it looks as if one of the dogs is now driving. Behind them, a minivan sporting a Casino Rama logo and filled with Asian senior citizens wallows through the corner, nearly goes up on two wheels, and barely misses hitting the ditch on the far side of the road. As the driver recovers control and wrenches the bus over to the right lane again, an old lady in the front holds out her hand and collects bets.

Second to last in the procession is a tiny yellow car with the ground clearance of a cockroach. The windows are tinted so dark it is impossible to see who is inside, but even five vehicles ahead I can hear its sound system booming out bass thuds and F-bombs to a hip-hop beat.

Bringing up the rear is a camper truck with boat trailer driven by a big guy in a plaid shirt, cowboy hat, and Viva Las Vegas sunglasses. His boat nearly takes out the stop sign.

Ski Trail Road runs parallel to Highway 11 for about eight klicks, then swerves west and peters out into what looks like a paved driveway. Potholes and washboard force us to slow to sixty. I look in the mirror. The lady in the Lexus is still just one car length off my rear bumper, now punching numbers into a Palm Pilot while talking on her phone.

Ski Trail road turns due north, pointing us back toward Gravenhurst. After several klicks I see a westbound road called Pooles coming up on the left. Better than that, there is a line of big trucks rolling south toward us at just the right distance that if I slow and turn at the last second, the posse will be completely cut off.

I execute a quick left just before the first of the southbound eighteen-wheelers arrives, blocking the entrance to Pooles Road behind me. We drive on alone, and our highway slowly turns into a residential road. Small country homes of indeterminate architecture give way to millionaire mansions on perfectly manicured grounds.

The speed limit drops to 50 kilometers per hour as we enter a new subdivision full of monster houses on tiny lots.

Pooles finally ends at a set of traffic lights at Franklin's Way. I have a choice: north or south.

"Which way?" I ask Pitt the Younger.

"Whatever," he replies with a scowl. The mere act of answering me has cost him a hundred points on his Game Boy.

As the light turns green, I hear a familiar throbbing noise behind us. I look in the mirror to see that my retinue has returned. The lady in the Casino Rama minivan is collecting bets again. I turn left, heading south toward Shanty Bay. We drive three klicks and then, by an unbelievable stroke of luck, I see Cundles Road straight ahead. I know Cundles leads to Essa, which in turn leads to Highway 27. We have found the promised road.

The posse knows this, too. Before I can change lanes, they get over to the right. I decide I need a coffee.

"Feel like getting something to eat?" I ask my son.

"Whatever," he says.

The light at Cundles is red. We sit in the center lane while one by one the cars in the convoy pull alongside and turn right. The lady in the Lexus appears to be nursing a baby as she goes past. The bike on the Volvo is straight again. The dogs and the kids in the Ford are asleep. The senior citizens in the minivan are exchanging money. Not even the chest-pounding boom-boom from the little yellow roadster can make them blink.

Not one person looks at me except for the big guy in the truck. As he draws up to turn right, he points his left index finger at me, then cocks his thumb and lets it fall like a pistol hammer. I nod. The last I see of him is the name on his boat.

"Thank U … Thank U, Very Much."

Steve Pitt has been a professional writer for more than thirty years. In 1980 he won a Periodical Distributors Author's Award for humour for an article that appeared in Harrowsmith magazine. In addition to being a writer, Steve Pitt has worked as a movie extra, army reserve soldier, dishwasher, farm hand, martial arts instructor, bartender, youth outreach worker, armoured truck guard, Yukon gold prospector, manager of a shelter for homeless men, goose rancher, lay minister, bar bouncer, resort cook, and stay-at-hom dad. You'll find him in cyberspace at www.stevepitt.ca.

Never Trust a Smiling Bear

Hey, are you smiling at me?

By Matt Jackson

For many Americans, Alaska is the final frontier: a land of fresh air, wide-open spaces and plentiful opportunity. It's a place where you can still lose yourself, and when you do get lost, it's often because you *choose* to be lost.

Of course, even when a person isn't outside communing with nature—ranging across the final frontier by boat, ATV or on foot—there is the distinct possibility that nature may come to them.

Suey Linzmeier of Sheep Creek, Alaska used to run a daycare for small children out of her home, which was located just south of Juneau. She was mystified that her son's papier-mâché castle, which the children loved playing with on the back porch, was slowly disintegrating. After repeated reminders to "play carefully" with the toy, her son became frustrated that the children weren't listening. It wasn't until a few days later that they realized a small black bear cub had been climbing the porch like a tree and chowing down on the papier-mâché treat.

The family also had a bear make off with an expensive bag of dog food, which it dropped after Suey and her husband pursued it into the forest.

None of these experiences, however, prepared her for the day in 2002 when a bear entered her house and used the bathroom to "beautify" itself. Suey had been baking all day long, preparing for a presentation on nutrition at a nearby town. The smell of fresh bread filled the air, and several large cheese pinwheels sat cooling on the counter.

Their home had a door that connected the house to the woodshed, which contained their large freezer. That particular afternoon Suey opened the door, walked out to the freezer to place some bread inside, and came face-to-face with a bear that had entered the woodshed through a second door on the left. She screamed and bolted out a third door, this one directly across from the second one. What Linzmeier didn't realize was that she had inadvertently left the first door ajar—the one that lead directly into their home.

As Suey ran around to the front of her house, the curious bear sauntered into the Linzmeier home through the open door. He proceeded to walk through the kitchen, down the hallway and into the family's bathroom.

When Suey entered through the front door she was shocked to see muddy paw prints tracking down her hallway. She pricked her ears and heard the bear rummaging around in the bathroom. She listened as it drank from the toilet, and after a few minutes she heard it climb into the shower stall. *What on earth?* she thought.

The next thing she knew she could hear the sound of running water. Was the bear taking a shower? Turns out he was. It was an older shower and the handles, when accidentally bumped, would easily turn the water on.

Eventually, the wet bear wandered out of the bathroom. Suey had by this time erected a wall of chairs and other furniture between her and the bruin so that it couldn't lunge at her directly. But attacking her didn't seem to be on its mind; instead, as the curious bear entered her kitchen again, she could have sworn it was *smiling* at her. Perhaps he had merely been cleaning himself up for dinner?

Linzmeier began shouting at the bruin, hoping that the loud noise would be enough to dissuade it from gorging itself on the rows of baked goods and cheese pinwheels. The bear sat down for several minutes and considered his options, but eventually the high-pitched screeching coming from Linzmeier was enough to prod it back out the door and into the woodshed.

Suey quickly shut and locked the door, but for the rest of the afternoon the bear stayed in her backyard. It would periodically come to the back door and wiggle and shake the doorknob, but the resourceful Linzmeier had by this time barricaded the entrance with the fridge. No dice, Mr. Bruin. No dinner for you.

While examining the bathroom later that day, Suey noticed mud smeared all over the bottom of her husband's bathrobe, which was hanging on the wall beside the shower. She likes to think the bear wiped his face on the bathrobe before showering—perhaps just one step of a process outlined in Mary Kay's guide to bear beautification.

Matt Jackson is an award-winning author and the editor of Never Trust a Smiling Bear. *Suey Linzmeier and her husband Scott now live in Sheridan, Oregon. They lived in Alaska for 25 years, and she still loves telling this story. It reminds her of the wild places and spaces of the 49th state.*

Bob of the Jungle

Hungry and bug bitten in the Amazon Basin.

By Robert Earle Howells

"We have only grubs to eat." Moises sounded apologetic about this.

"Great!" I said, and meant it.

I'd had it with hunger. I'd had it with wet. My own scent offended me. My arms ached from waving off kamikaze flotillas of mosquitoes. I'd had it with sweat bees, desperately in love with my sodden leather boots, clouds of them swirling around my feet at every stride. I was a starved sweat machine, a giant itch, a sleep-deprived gringo who couldn't even catch a guinea pig for dinner.

But I'd developed a yen for grubs. On a survival trip in the deep green heart of Peru's upper Amazon rainforest, necessity and reason cut some weird deals in your brain. You learn to like beetle larva.

Actually, grubs aren't bad. The wiggly, juicy larvae of beetles living out their pre-pupating days inside the nuts of moriche palm trees are tasty and convenient. Just be sure to chew the writhing little suckers (a smidgen of crunch, then a creamy release), or you'll become a beetle-breeding facility.

Munch your grubs. That was one of numerous lessons of jungle life conveyed to me by Moises Chavez—jungle guide, rainforest wizard, and often-taciturn midwife to gringos seeking rebirth through privation in the jungle. A man I'd come to admire, to hate, and to love, depending upon the status of my stomach at any given moment.

I'd descended into this atavistic state in a short period of time—just a few days into a jungle survival week offered by a remote lodge on the Tahuayo River, an Amazon tributary about sixty river miles south of Iquitos.

All I'd need, they told me, was a machete.

As one ordinarily prideful about preparation, the act of jettisoning nearly every piece of survival equipment offended my instinctive desire to live a long life. But what's more liberating than abandoning one's scruples? Bob of the Jungle: a lean, keen, bug-eating denizen of the tropical woodlands. Sign me up.

Moises met me at the airport in the jungle city of Iquitos. We boated about three hours up the Amazon, then a subsequent hour up the Tahuayo River to the lodge. The place was a deep-jungle fantasy. A lattice of cedar walkways soared on stilts twenty feet above the river floodplain. Breezes blew through screened-in rooms with high ceilings and elegant exposed beams. The mess hall opened onto a gorgeous river view. I fell easily into lodge life, rousing myself off the hammock for stretches of bird watching, monkey gawking, and piranha fishing, punctuated by three square meals a day.

Moises's job as chief guide at Tahuayo Lodge is to run activities for the guests. I saw the slight, intense, and laconic Moises as something of a jungle sylph—a man eerily in harmony with the mysteries of the rainforest, who walked lightly and easily through its ill-defined corridors, calling up its denizens as if whistling for Fido. Indeed, he was a man who read the inscrutable green of the jungle as effortlessly as I might the food aisles at a Safeway.

Moises gleaned his survival smarts during a childhood spent in Indian villages deep in the Peruvian jungle, where his late father, Gerenaldo, had been a teacher to indigenous tribes. Born in the Yagua Indian village of Huanana on the Napo River, Moises took lessons in the thatched-roof schoolhouses that his father built, and participated in all the rites of growing up native. If his pals were going spearfishing, Moises went too. If they were extracting curare from the bacaba palm for poison blowgun darts, Moises did likewise. When ill, he visited the local *curandero*, or shaman.

"I'm all the time very curious as a boy," Moises told me, "and live with other boys like animals." (Moises speaks an endearing pidgin that conveys deep intelligence.) "I see when we hunt and fish how they move through the jungle."

Paul Beaver—Floridian, lapsed biologist, and owner of Tahuayo Lodge—heard about Moises through the adventure-travel grapevine. "I was like a struggling sports franchise willing to pay astronomical sums to a star player. I treated Moises as a free agent and persuaded him to come work with me."

On the eve of our jungle-survival departure, I packed the lightest one-week pack in history: a change of clothes, headlamp, poncho, a bit of DEET, mosquito netting, and a water bottle. Moises and I pulled out early in the morning and motored upstream, where the Tahuayo quickly narrowed and became shallow. Its tannic brown turned a shiny obsidian, and the rainforest curtain fell around us.

After an hour, we saw few settlements and no villages; after two hours, nothing but jungle. When we ditched the boat, we were on the northern edge of the two-million-acre Tamshiyacu-Tahuayo Reserve, more than a full day's journey by fast boat from the nearest incandescent lightbulb.

I have no idea how far we walked through the lowland jungle that first day, machetes slashing the undergrowth, because Moises took his role as lecturer so seriously. We'd halt constantly. Moises who carried no binoculars, would motion for us to stop, point into the mottled canopy 150 feet overhead and declare, "Squirrel monkeys," and I'd spend the next five minutes with my binoculars trying to dial in even a glimpse of the chattering creatures. "In the trees," he'd add, with no note of sarcasm.

Moises is a small, wiry man—about five feet, three inches tall, and weighing perhaps 135 pounds. His gait appears nonchalant. His shoulders are slightly stooped, and his feet seem to shuffle. But they aren't really shuffling; they're skimming the ground a micron above the surface, and they rarely rustle a leaf or snap a twig. He seems never to look down. His eyes are free to spot every monkey, toucan, tree rat, and sloth in the reserve.

I tried to be a good student of the jungle. It wasn't easy. To my eyes, everything was homogeneously green and arrayed in a cutthroat fashion. Vines dangled from every branch; strangler figs formed spirals that would eventually squeeze the life out of huge hardwoods; and bromeliads sprouted like bright red carbuncles from trunks and branches.

Besides his nature lessons, Moises was given to sudden proclamations, which were often non sequiturs. After one stretch of silence, he announced, "The jungle is a very big place, but here is not dangerous. With a good guide, nothing going to happen to you."

"I'm glad of that, Moises, but what about lunch?" A few basic differences between us were beginning to emerge. Moises seemed never to eat or drink. I was always hungry and thirsty. Moises could see everything. I could see nothing. And—at first, anyway—I thought Moises had no sense of humor.

"Can we bag a tapir or something? I'm starved."

"We eat fish. Later."

Okie dokie. I'll be the guy wobbling along behind you.

At midday we arrived at our first campsite in a clearing disconcertingly near a swamp. Fertile mosquito turf, I astutely observed, but I kept that to myself, too.

We set about building a *tambo*, an open-sided hut, which was a matter of hacking down a forest of small trees for uprights and beams, lashing framework together with strips of machimango bark, and using strands of tamshi vine to tie down a million or so overlapping palm fronds to form the A-shaped roof. For the final touches, we threw down a thin bed of palm leaves for a floor and strung up our individual mosquito nets. (If you think that final bit of luxury sounds like cheating, *you* go sleep beside a lowland Amazon swamp without one.)

All of this was taking place minus the benefit of sustenance. (Dammit, Moises, no more science lectures before dinner! Let's just get to the fishing hole!) So when Moises paused and pointed yet again, I nearly barked out my irritation—until I realized he was gesturing toward a big downfall of orange, pulpy fruit called anahuayo. They were fetid, bruised by their long fall, and well picked over by monkeys. I sucked a sweet lunch out of the fallen rot.

We reached a still, muddy stream. How did we expect to fish this opaque bit of murk? Easy. In the practical fashion of the jungle people, we'd poison the suckers. We cut bundles of roots from the barbasco plant, smashed them with thick branches to release their toxins, and swished them in the water. In twenty minutes, two dozen stupefied fish surfaced. They still had to be speared, though—a skill I couldn't begin to master. Moises's success rate was a cool 100 percent. He racked up a huge catch, scrawny and bony but tasty when smoked over a tropical-wood fire.

At first, hunger and various other plagues made this jungle—and Moises—easier to respect than love. In my grumpy state, I started viewing Moises as a show-off who was taking delight in showing up the gringo rube. Not that he did so overtly—but when he would halt a march to proclaim, "Bob, now you gonna learn to make the backpack for fruit," I'd want to say, "Moises, I'm hungry. Weave the frigging thing yourself."

So much for Bob of the Jungle.

There were plagues beyond mere starvation to contend with. Of these, vermin reigned supreme. The air of the lowland jungle was an ether of mosquitoes. I'd packed the strongest DEET-based repellent I could find, 110 percent or so—but in the intense humidity of the jungle, I'd sweat away each application in short order, and my flesh soon belonged to the bugs again. One day, Moises showed me the jungle prophylactic for biting bugs. Simple: just stick your fist into a nest of brown termites and let them crawl over your arms and shoulders. When I was sufficiently infested, I ground them into my skin, releasing a woodsy cologne. It seemed to work … for about ten minutes.

I was only safe inside my mosquito netting, surrounded by the desperate din of flying cannibals. But in the day-night equality of the tropics, one generally had to heed nature's call at least once in twelve hours. I'd emerge and endeavor to do my duty amid a flailing of arms (you can guess where the critters were headed). Then I'd bring a fleet of mosquitoes back into the confines of my net and spend the next forty-five minutes performing ritual murders.

My feet ached. You can't sit down in the rainforest, because the floor of the jungle belongs to army ants, and the troops quickly swarm over any limb or *derriere* in their reach.

Lack of sleep plagued me. It wasn't fear of death that caused my insomnia; it was the noise. The salient truth of the jungle is a constant state of rot. Something is always falling, breaking, or creaking. Fruits and nuts 150 feet overhead make a tremendous clatter on their way through the canopy. Nocturnal footsteps rustle the forest floor ominously. Jaguar? Tapir? (More likely toads, Moises told me later.) It was like trying to sleep while someone rattled your doorknob every few minutes.

We slept in our swampside tambo the next few nights, and I spent my days tailing Moises, gleaning jungle wisdom and searching for calorie sources. Moises in action was dazzling. "Here's where the tapir crossed the river," he'd observe. ("Was that to get to the other side, Moises?" No laugh.) "Here's an armadillo trail … there's a jaguar track … we'll eat this snail for lunch."

For all its perils and its skinflint reluctance to offer up anything to eat, it dawned on me after a few days that I was growing to like the jungle. For one thing, I was no longer constantly hungry. (It helped that we found a fallen palm trunk, a source of larger, even juicier grubs: writhing babes the length of an index finger and the girth of a big toe. I downed the jumbos raw and with relish.)

I found myself increasingly eager to penetrate the jungle's inscrutability, and more accepting of Moises's own. So when he announced, "We gotta cut this tree down," I asked no questions and happily hacked down a 75-foot palm. At about Foot 73, the trunk was slender, tender, and deliciously edible: heart of palm. We even found some lemony cocona fruit to drizzle over our evening's shaved-heart-of-palm salad.

"We move to terra firma today," Moises announced the morning of our fifth day. The nearest terra firma (land higher than the seasonal flood zone) required a half-day hike up and over a ridge. The jungle here was denser, more textbook primeval. Everything grew bigger. Bushwhacking was difficult. But what could be cooler for an American lad raised on jungle fantasies than to hack his way with a machete through impenetrable rainforest?

As we began to raise a new tambo that afternoon, we both sensed imminent rain. "Woman rain," Moises announced five minutes before the deluge. "When woman cry, it all day." The sky became a waterfall, but it was a relief to feel a ten-degree drop in air temperature and to grab a shower as we worked.

The next morning, over an absence of breakfast, Moises announced, "Today we gonna make the trap." Picturing a bit of subterfuge that would snare tasty fodder for a lunchtime barbecue, I began, under orders, hacking posts and gathering palm fronds. After long hours of sweaty labor, we had constructed an installation Cristo would be proud to claim. This was landscape sculpture—a four-foot-high palm-frond fence stretching 100 feet along a ridge. Two narrow openings were sprung with huge logs that would thwack any beast seeking a way through.

"What exactly do we hope to capture?" I asked Moises.

"Rat."

"Rat? Moises, we've fenced off half the Amazon basin to pummel a rat to death?"

Moises smiled. "Guinea pig, actually. Or could be snake. I no like, but we have to eat. Jungle people say it bad luck not to eating what you catch." He meant it, but he was obviously having some fun jabbing me.

"And when might we expect this dinner rodent or serpent to offer his demise?"

Late at night, of course. There'd be only a few bony fish for dinner.

When we made our rounds the next morning, our installation had snared nothing. "Not long enough," was Moises's explanation.

"The jungle people, they making trap many longer."

This observation led Moises into a stirring and truthful soliloquy: "Nothing easy in the jungle. People think they reading a book, they coming here and understand. It's not true."

No such illusions on my part. Visions of the rainforest as a benevolent kingdom come had long since been starved, sweated, and itched out of me. Still, all the necessities of life were there; they were just a bit beyond easy access. The jungle's generosity lay in its abundance, not in convenience.

Did it matter that we'd caught nothing in our contraption? Did not a long day's shared labor in building it bring us closer together? Were we not laughing now? Well, yes. Maybe surviving the jungle really meant enduring its hardships as friends. Maybe.

But I was still hungry.

Robert Earle Howells won the Lowell Thomas Travel Journalist of the Year silver award in 2009. He has been surviving adventures for more than thirty years as a writer for Outside, National Geographic Adventure, *and* Men's Journal. *For excruciating close-ups of his grub-eating adventures in the Amazon, check out his rainforest documentary at* **www.snagfilms.com/films/title/the_ rainforest_wisdom_of_moises_chavez/**

Toyotas Don't Float

And other lessons learned while exploring the Yukon.

By Don Wilkinson

For a number of years my friend Geoff and I had taken the same trip deep into the Yukon's Ruby Range in search of the elusive Yukon moose. Oh sure, we often spotted some, but shooting them would have entailed far more work then we were willing to expend. So we told our friends that all we ever saw were females. They believed us and we were never obliged to shoot anything. Everyone simply assumed that we were lousy hunters, which was probably true anyway.

We tended to view these trips more as exploratory camping expeditions, during which we searched for ever-new ways to destroy Geoff's 4x4 trucks. We never once took one of my vehicles. I knew better. And fortunately, Geoff isn't one to learn from past mistakes—at least not when it came to listening to my advice. He and I spent a couple of pleasant decades destroying large numbers of his vehicles. He never once declined my suggestion to bring his vehicle, and rarely did he hesitate when I told him to "Go for it!"

It never seemed to matter if it was a deep river crossing or a cliff that we needed to drive up or down. Geoff would generally accept my assurances that "It'll be fine," and drive cheerfully over the cliff or plunge gleefully into a fast-moving river. He simply never learned. Never! Our wives eventually put a stop to it; if they hadn't, we'd both be happily burning, rolling, or drowning his vehicles to this day.

One year we decided to bring a friend along on our trip. Lenny was a short, roundish little guy who shared our love of camping and trail driving. We decided to take him to our favorite spot for "not hunting," a steep-walled valley in the Gladstone River Valley, about seventy kilometers up the east arm of Kluane Lake.

There's a fair-sized grizzly population in the valley, but we never messed with them, and up to that point they hadn't messed with us—though I suppose just once would be enough.

The trail into the valley begins near the abandoned mining town of Silver City, and is easy to miss if you're not paying attention. True to form, we weren't paying attention, missed the trail, and spent an extra hour searching for it. It didn't help that we disagreed on the exact location of the trailhead. It turned out that neither location was anywhere near where it actually was located, a fact that we should have remembered from every other year we'd missed it.

Eventually we found the trailhead—hidden behind a large shrub—and proceeded to drive down the trail through a dense pine forest and a couple of spruce swamps, plus the occasional stream crossing as the waterways rushed hell-bent through sheer-walled gorges.

We used the winch repeatedly, but still managed to make the first leg of the journey in record-breaking, back-breaking, and truck-breaking time. After three hours we had traveled sixteen kilometers, so we stopped for some lunch and coffee while our backsides regained partial blood circulation.

After we left our lunch spot, the trail became more difficult. We started the climb up and along the side of a mountain that towered over a large lake. The trail had been carved from the side of the cliff twenty years earlier by a D7 bulldozer and hadn't been touched since. The mountain's shale face tended to suffer frequent landslides and avalanches.

Our truck was about six feet wide; the widest spot on the trail was less. In some areas it was much, much less. For those stretches, we had to drive the inside wheels up onto the cliff face and scuttle across like a crab, hoping that the trail didn't narrow even further. At one point Geoff walked ahead to guide me as I drove up and over some fallen rock slabs that teetered at the edge of the precipice.

Geoff got me to stop so he could take some pictures, no doubt to prove how stupid we were. Lenny sat in the truck and gazed vacantly out at the sheer drop-off.

Neither Geoff nor I could ever be accused of being altruistic when it came to each other's safety: although it was Geoff's truck, he always made me drive whenever it might be somewhat dangerous. It was a sort of symbiotic relationship. He risked his trucks, but he let me risk my neck whenever the going got particularly dangerous.

We safely negotiated the cliff face, and after several more hours of bone-shaking, teeth-rattling, bladder-busting fun, we finally arrived at the spot where the trail plunges over the rim and descends into the basin of the Gladstone River. Geoff reached down, shoved the gearshift into 4 HIGH, and gave a fear-tinged giggle that even had Lenny doubting the wisdom of the trip. We plunged over the edge.

After a few terror-filled moments—during which the truck slid sideways on the steep incline—we arrived safely at the bottom. We inched our way across the valley floor to the stream's edge, where we came to a shuddering halt.

Something wasn't right. The gentle stream we knew from previous trips was now a raging torrent, and the shallow section we normally used for crossing was now completely washed away.

Geoff and I got out and stood looking down at last year's tire tracks, which disappeared into the floodwaters. Forty feet away, we could make out the tracks as they emerged from the furious white water.

I hesitated … but what the heck? It wasn't my truck!

Geoff looked a little green, but there was no way he would admit to being scared. He looked at me. I looked at him. I shrugged my shoulders and said those four fateful words that have gotten us into so much trouble in the past: "Let's go for it!"

Just for good measure, I threw in "What can go wrong?"

We climbed back into the truck. Geoff leaned over, pulled the gearshift into 4 LOW, and with a fatalistic shrug, plunged over the bank and into the stream.

As we edged into the current, the truck stayed on course—at least for the first few meters. Icy meltwater hammered at the door panels and swirled higher and higher toward my open window. (I was keeping it open in case things went south; the last thing I wanted was to be stuck in a sinking truck without an exit strategy.)

We could hear and sometimes feel large rocks smash into the underside of the truck. The occasional rock would strike hard enough to jolt the vehicle and momentarily slew us sideways. The truck sunk deeper and water began washing across the hood, beating against the windshield. An errant tree passed by and ripped off one of the truck's wiper blades.

I was starting to get worried, but as long as the engine continued running and the river didn't get any deeper, we would remain in fine shape. Soon the front end of the truck disappeared beneath the water's surface, and the river began pouring through my open window. It didn't take long for it to fill the cab. A few seconds later the truck gasped its final breath.

The truck swung sideways in the current and threatened to roll over, drowning anybody who was trapped inside. I was out that window so fast I left burn marks on the window frame. Geoff emerged a few seconds later, and Lenny popped out the rear window like a fat little champagne cork. The strange thing was that his window was only a foot square, and an average cross section of Lenny is considerably larger than that. We never did figure out how he made it through that tiny opening.

The three of us stood in the back of the truck as it floated downstream, pushed along by the forty-knot current. As the riverbank rushed past, we calmly took stock of our situation and noticed a number of things that might not be of much benefit to us.

First, we were soaking wet, half-frozen, and floating down a river in the back of a stalled Toyota that was drifting who-knows-where—a Toyota that seemed to be sinking ever lower as we called each other bad names and tried to lay the blame on each other.

Second, our rifles, shells, wallets, and my camera were still in the flooded truck cab.

Third, and perhaps most important, so was most of our food, my smokes, and every match and lighter we possessed. Luckily, my smokes and a lighter had been tucked up in the sun visor, and I was able to rescue them by prying open the sunroof.

We lit cigarettes and stood in the back contemplating our next move. I was in full denial when the truck ground to a screeching halt, trapped in the bowels of an enormous mass of driftwood and deadfall timber. The sharp end of a broken tree had driven itself clean through the rear quarter panel of the truck.

Lenny panicked and jumped onto the pile of driftwood, then jumped from tree to tree until he had reached the shore. Geoff and I heaved our gear to him as the truck settled lower and lower into the water, and then scrambled to the relative safety of the logs just as the truck slipped gently beneath the waves.

We watched forlornly as the headlights and roof lights winked out, one after the other, six feet below the surface.

Things got worse. We soon realized that we were now trapped on the wrong side of the river. Moreover, we had no rifles to defend ourselves from bears; it was getting cold and dark; we were shivering violently; and we no longer had a truck to get us seventy kilometers back to the Alaska Highway.

We decided that a good cup of coffee would at least warm us up, so we gathered some deadfall and built a small fire on the shore. Because someone had prudently thought to use backpacks and duffel bags, my spare clothes were fairly dry. I changed into my dry duds and waited for the coffee to brew and things to improve somehow. The coffee was dreadful and nothing else improved, including our tempers.

As we drank the vile brew, the three of us began discussing a rescue plan. Geoff and Lenny wanted to walk the seventy kilometers out to the Alaska Highway in the dark, and then flag down a passing tourist for a ride into town. This was assuming, of course, that we could find our way across the river again.

It was around this time that I remembered Kluane Lake was not far—probably about three kilometers—and suggested that if we hiked to the shore, we could light some signal fires. Hopefully somebody driving the road on the far side of the lake would see our fire and come to the rescue.

We hiked upstream through the woods until we eventually found a series of rocks and logs that allowed us to cross the river. To discourage any grizzlies that might be lurking in the area, we shouted at each other a lot. After we had staggered around in the dark for an hour or so, the forest opened up and we stepped onto the rocky, windswept shores of Kluane Lake. We scurried around, gathering driftwood and piling it into gigantic heaps.

As we all knew, three fires in a row indicates danger or trouble, and is universally known as such throughout the world. What we weren't aware of at the time was that the three fires—when seen from across the lake—lined up perfectly and simply looked like one very large fire. (Albeit a large enough fire that anybody could have felt its heat from the far side of the lake.)

We stayed up half the night making sure those fires didn't go out, with nothing to show for it but three huge piles of ash. After a while we gave up and settled down on the rocky shore to get what sleep we could. A long walk in the morning seemed to be our destiny after all.

Shortly after we had fallen asleep, we were wakened by the sound of a motorboat approaching from across the lake. The owner of a highway lodge had spotted our fires hours before, but being a practical man, had waited until the bar closed before coming to see what was up. We were just grateful to see him at all.

After laughing at our stupidity and general predicament, he offered to take us across the lake, where he would feed us and put us up for the night.

And what became of Geoff's Toyota? We went back a week later to get it, experiencing another series of misadventures along the way.

But that is a story for another day.

Although he no longer lives in the Yukon, Don Wilkinson spent 26 years residing in the Land of the Midnight Sun. Some of his fondest memories are those of getting lost while happily destroying his and other peoples' vehicles. Don is the author of a soon-to-be-published travel guide to the Czech Republic and is the humor columnist for Canadian Woodworking Magazine.

Monkey Business

He sure looks like a monkey.

By Sarah Lolley

The whole disastrous side trip to Dalat had been my idea.

I'm a sucker for visiting places that I've read about in books, and Dalat, located way up in the Central Highlands of Vietnam, made an appearance in the Graham Greene novel *A Quiet American*. It wasn't on the itinerary for our four-month backpacking tour of Southeast Asia, but I pleaded with my boyfriend Jack to indulge my curiosity. Graciously, he did.

As soon as we arrived, it became clear that I had made a mistake. The place held little appeal. It was cold and rainy. Our hotel was an oppressive concrete block that echoed with the footsteps of its only guests: us. I felt awful.

My guilt only intensified when we toured the botanical gardens, again at my suggestion. They were as scrappy as a miniature golf course, despite the inflated ticket price for foreigners. The only thing of interest was the monkey enclosure, where five mangy simians hopped around inside individual cages.

As we approached, one cheeky monkey climbed the bars of his cage to our eye level. Jack laughed in surprise and leaned in to get a better look at the monkey. The monkey leaned in to get a better look at Jack. The two stared at each other for a moment. Then, with a flash of his small paw, the monkey reached through the bars, snatched the sunglasses off Jack's face, and retreated to the middle of its cage.

The sunglasses weren't expensive—we had paid fifteen dollars for them at a gas station in the Australian outback—but Jack loved them, mainly because of the cheesy race car flames down the sides. We watched glumly as the monkey chewed on one of the arms of the sunglasses. When he tried to put them on, they fell off his head onto the dirt floor of the cage.

Great, I thought. *Now I've caused my boyfriend to lose his favourite eyewear.*

"Maybe someone has a key," I suggested lamely. The thick layer of rust covering the lock implied that this was unlikely.

Jack shrugged. "It's worth a shot," he said, and disappeared around a corner in the direction of the ticket booth.

I watched as the monkey opened and closed the arms of the sunglasses, cursing him silently.

Then I remembered the banana in my backpack and a plan was hatched. It was as if the dreary skies had parted and a beam of inspiration had shone down on me. I knew with calm certainty that my plan would work.

The sound of my bag unzipping caught the monkey's attention. When I extracted the banana, he lost all interest in the sunglasses, dropping them in the dirt in order to jump up to my level again. He stretched out his little paw. *Aha!* I thought. *I was right.*

"Now, listen here," I addressed the primate, imitating the voice of a stern librarian. "You are an intelligent animal and what I am proposing is a simple trade. You have something I want," I said, pointing at the sunglasses.

The monkey looked down at them, then back at me.

"And I have something you want." I held up the banana.

I could almost see the wheels turning inside the monkey's head. His expression was one of great deliberation. *The sunglasses are shiny and new*, I imagined him thinking. *Then again, they don't taste of anything much. Plus, my ears are too small to hold them up...*

As the monkey raised his paw toward the banana again, I brimmed with self-confidence. *This is totally going to work*, I enthused to myself. *I am brilliant!*

A young Vietnamese woman wandered over. She watched me talking to the monkey for a few moments, and then comprehension spread across her face. She called out to a Vietnamese man, who came rushing over.

I smiled at them smugly. *That's right!* I thought, proudly. *Come and see how industrious we Canadian travelers are!*

"You want the banana," I told the monkey in clearly enunciated English. "And I want the sunglasses." I pointed alternately at the sunglasses and the banana. The monkey looked from one object to the other.

This time, when the monkey looked back up at me, his expression was blank. It caught me off guard. His face no longer reflected sage consideration; he just looked like a monkey.

A crack formed in the bedrock of my poise.

A group of five Vietnamese men in business suits ambled over. A rapid-fire exchange ensued between the couple and the businessmen. Two of the men started giggling.

I tried to ignore them. I would get the sunglasses back, I reassured myself. I would make it right again.

"Look, you want the banana, right?" I pleaded with the monkey. "So just give me the sunglasses! It's easy!"

This time, the monkey ignored me completely. He glanced over at my Vietnamese audience and scratched his bum.

Shame started to burn around my heart. I wasn't going to get the sunglasses back after all, I realized.

You IDIOT! I cursed myself. Why on earth had I thought I could communicate with a monkey? Why had I insisted on coming to this stupid town? Why did I always think I knew best?

At that very moment, the monkey dropped to the ground, picked up the sunglasses, and lumbered over to the side of the cage. He then extended his little monkey arm outside the bars and dropped them at my feet.

The businessmen stopped giggling. The Vietnamese woman gasped. All eyes, including the monkey's, were on me. The monkey stretched his paw through the bars for the banana.

Was it a trick? Drawing a shaky breath, I crouched down and retrieved the sunglasses.

I'm ashamed to admit that for a brief second I did think about leaving the monkey high and dry, as revenge for the humiliation I had nearly suffered. But it wasn't his fault, and fair was fair. So I placed the banana in his tiny paw.

"Sarah!" Jack's voice shouted behind me.

I turned to see him approaching, two groundskeepers in tow. I smiled victoriously, holding up the sunglasses for all to see.

Sarah Lolley has travelled to 34 countries on five continents, and has spent time living in France, Jamaica, Scotland, and Australia. Her travel articles and personal essays have appeared in The Globe and Mail, ELLE Canada, Reader's Digest, The Toronto Star and Up! *magazine. In all her travels, Sarah has never met a wheeling-and-dealing monkey that she didn't like.*

Paddling as a Parental Tool

Or how to ruin your son's life for the rest of eternity.

By John Iannotti

Our family started paddling when my three kids were in their teens. One of our favorite family adventures was to paddle down Loyalsock Creek in our home state of Pennsylvania on weekends. We made it an annual family tradition, with picnics along the thirty-five kilometers of river that we usually covered. So when my oldest son Jeff and I needed to work out a conflict, it seemed appropriate that I use the paddling experience to build a bond between us.

A little background: Jeff was fourteen or fifteen at the time, and very conservative in his behavior. He was not a risk taker; in fact, he could easily be described as introverted. On the flip side, I am naturally gregarious and rarely see a risk not worth taking. We were at odds over discipline relating to some of his chores, but I don't remember exactly what the issue was. After all, he's now forty-two with three sons of his own, one of whom is very much like me.

We put in above Higgins Camp and floated down the river, arguing along the way about which parts of the creek to run. I wanted to hit all the big waves, while my son preferred to avoid them. Bonding was not going so well.

As we approached the swimming hole before a rapid called *Last Chance Saloon*, we faced a very big decision. To the right was my target: a narrow, fast-curving section of river with a large wave train beneath a rock wall. To the left was a very shallow section that rippled over small rocks for a bumpy but simple ride down.

Jeff tried desperately to paddle the front of our sixteen-foot Coleman canoe to the left, while I used rudder strokes to overpower him. There was no evidence of bonding at this time, and any witness would have seen an epic battle taking place.

As any canoeist would know, I easily won the battle for direction. But here's the thing: my son's strokes had left us broadside to the channel, and as we entered the Class III section I lost control of the canoe. We became airborne on the first of the sizeable waves, which quickly swamped the canoe and dumped us into the whitewater. We swallowed water as we rode the rapids down the remainder of the chute and into a swimming hole.

To our surprise there were a large number of teenagers frolicking in the swimming hole, including several classmates from Jeff's high school. We washed up on the shore across from them. My son had lost various items and had to dive for them in the swimming hole at the base of the rapids. Meanwhile, I bent over and began bailing out the water-filled boat.

When my son finally came back to the canoe, he looked very humiliated and very angry. He told me that we had to leave immediately. The teens across the river had stopped whatever they were doing and were now gathered together laughing and pointing at us; I guessed that their hysterical laughter was making him uncomfortable.

To prove my competency and regain some respect, I stood up in the back of the canoe as we paddled away. For some reason, the laughter increased. When I sat down and felt the very cold seat, I knew why. My bathing suit had torn open at the back and I had been mooning the crowd for several minutes while I was bailing out the boat. My standing in the canoe was an unexpected encore.

When I told Jeff, he gave me a look that turned from horror to extreme anger, then faded slowly to fear as he contemplated facing his classmates at school. He paddled harder than I thought was possible until we had rounded the bend and slipped out of sight of the applauding high school kids.

We rarely talk about that day without his face showing a range of emotions. I still enjoy telling the story, though.

John Iannotti is a retired engineer and manager who has been active in youth activities all his adult life. Having lost his father a month after birth he appreciated the importance of having a dad, so he got involved with Boy Scouts, Big Brothers and Big Sisters. He served in all capacities, but prefers the fieldwork, like camping in the jungles of Panama with his troops and paddling on the rivers of eastern Pennsylvania.

Masters of Mayhem

Finding danger in the likeliest of places.

By Greg Simison

Teenagers are often loath to listen to advice, no matter how well intentioned, but when I was young I uncharacteristically took one suggestion to heart. After expressing a desire to be a writer and see as much of this country as I could, I was advised by a veteran traveler to learn a trade in the hospitality business. With the high turnover of staff in most hotels, you will always be assured of work should you find yourself cash-strapped and in the middle of nowhere—a place and financial condition in which I've often found myself. Acting on that recommendation was probably one of the few intelligent things I've done in my life.

Over the next few years I learned hotel front desk procedures. I also learned that the most important person to suck up to in the accommodation sector is not the general manager, but the chef. Make friends with the chef and you will never go hungry. His edible mistakes will regularly make their way to the registration desk. Having bravely sampled the failed experiments of many new short-order cooks, I've learned firsthand that the possibility of death by food poisoning is remote.

The possibility of death at the hands of guests is another matter.

Several years ago I was working as a shift supervisor at a hotel in the Okanagan Valley. One evening I found myself staring at a reservation for ten rooms booked by a "sports team." It lacked a cash deposit or a credit card guarantee. I pointed this out to the rookie clerk I was training that evening and reminded her that such bookings are routinely released at six o'clock. "As of six, these suckers are history," I pompously announced.

No sooner had these words escaped my mouth than I heard the roar of a large number of motorcycles approaching at somewhere near the speed of light. A nanosecond later, a dozen Harley-Davidson bikes pulled up at the hotel's front entrance. My stomach sank; my sports team had arrived.

I refused to dwell too long on which sports they might be involved in, though my mind proffered fleeting images of murals I'd seen in Mayan temples, depicting soccer-like games that used human heads as balls. I quietly gave thanks to whatever god— Mayan or otherwise—who had arranged for this group to arrive before six and not an hour later to find their rooms gone.

I spent the next few minutes checking these guests in while trying not to stare at the leather jackets advertising "Hells Angels." (Leather jackets, I might add, that were stretched to their limits around large biker bellies. Those processed cowhides certainly hadn't fit the original owners that snugly.)

All in all, it went well. The bikers politely provided gold or platinum American Express cards, or paid cash in advance.

The only hitch occurred when the rookie clerk attempted to help me by cheerily announcing, "Welcome to Vernon, gentlemen,"—and then adding after a short pause, "Geez, haven't you guys ever heard of Weight Watchers?"

My life flashed before my eyes. On the other hand, *I* hadn't said it. I only hoped her parents could handle it when I called to inform them of their daughter's tragic demise.

Instead of the expected outburst, the bikers just smiled warmly and asked where they might park their bikes. "Wherever you want," I told them. "Around the indoor pool, in the lobby, the elevator … anywhere."

Once they were settled I wandered outside to where several hundred thousand dollars' worth of bikes now formed an expensive obstacle course for anyone attempting to enter the hotel. A gang member, left outside to guard the fleet, was smiling and helpfully fielding any questions asked by a small crowd of gawkers that had gathered. His hospitable attitude didn't seem quite right to me; the guy sounded like a typical public-relations man. And there was something else that bothered me: the bikes were spotless. Not a single mud splatter, bloodstain, or body part dangling from a tailpipe. These were Hells Angels?

Several hours later I was still musing over these new-image Angels when I took my dinner break in the hotel coffee shop. Shortly after I sat down, a group of them took a seat in the booth across from me—in the non-smoking section, believe it or not. Their riding clothes had been set aside in favor of jogging pants,

T-shirts (still sporting the chapter's death's-head logo), and $200 Adidas or Nike running shoes. I was reminded of the previous month's hairdressing convention.

And their dinner choices did little to dispel this image, both for me and for the trembling waitress who was taking their orders. The orders went something like this:

Rocko: "I'd like the braised garlic chicken breast with a Caesar salad, please."

Scarface: "Gosh, Rocko, are you sure about that? You know how garlic gives you gas."

Thumbless Jack: "I think I'll go for the shrimp cocktail with a garden salad. But can you leave the sauce off my shrimp? It's way too rich. I can barely squeeze into my leathers these days."

Stomper: "Hey, tell me about it. I should lend you my ThighMaster. It really improved my muscle tone."

What is this? I thought. No one ordering raw meat? Bikers who want to avoid the loud discharges of gas that usually announce their presence and non-conformity? ThighMasters? Muscle tone?

You know, I can handle getting older, though grudgingly, but I'd like a few things in this world to remain constant. Is there any group out there that hasn't fallen under the spell of political correctness? Not one of these bikers had attempted to grope a waitress, or even hinted at anything that could be remotely construed as sexual harassment. They'd been in the building for hours and I'd yet to see a drop of blood spilled, a bike driven through the front doors, or weapons of any sort wielded. To be honest, I was feeling a little disappointed. My only hope was that later, once they got heavily into the white wine and piña coladas at the bar, there might be a confrontation of some sort. It would have been entertaining (in a dark kind of way) to see them leap to their feet and attack the other patrons. But from what I'd seen so far, I imagined any possible confrontation would be little more than a brief skirmish involving tossed swizzle sticks and tiny umbrellas.

By nine o'clock I realized nothing of this sort was going to happen, though I had the feeling that somewhere, deep inside, the Hells Angels that Hunter S. Thompson had described must still exist. I decided that to salvage some semblance of the world as it once had been, I would have to take matters into my own hands. So I walked outside, nodded at the two leather-clad giants guarding the bikes, announced it was Harley washing time, and unzipped.

That did the trick. I regained consciousness a few seconds later and realized that what I thought was my pounding heart was actually a large boot repeatedly making contact with my abdomen. The old world was restored.

"Thank you," I muttered through blood-spattered lips.

No sooner were those words out of my mouth than I saw another body intervening, shoving my attacker back and yelling, " No, Axe. Stop! Don't do it! Your anger-management counselor will be furious!"

Of course, I'm just kidding. That last incident didn't really happen.

But I want to assure you that all these guys are as mean and tough as they ever were. Believe that. Please believe that, because the guy who was kneeling on my chest that night vowed that if

I ever described them as anything less than vicious, he would be back to pin my neck to the floor with the switchblade he was holding to my throat.

Well, he told me it was a switchblade. I've still got a vague feeling it was just the sharp edge of a ThighMaster.

Greg Simison is a poet, playwright and former newspaper columnist who lives in Moose Jaw, Saskatchewan. Despite having had four books published, rumours persist that, like his city, he doesn't really exist. He's recently started believing this himself.

Pains, Trains and Wildfires

Sometimes you need to see how bad things can get before you see how good they really are.

By Neil McKinnon

This is the story of how my wife and I decided to rekindle our relationship, which had become painful and unexciting as a result of raising a family and working long hours—myself in a repetitive business in Calgary, and she as a teacher of small children in a rural elementary school.

Our marriage had not always been bland. Once, like a shirt drying on a line, it had blown into many different shapes—but when the breeze stopped, it always fell back to what it was. At one time, it had been soft and wonderful. In those days she called me Twinkle Butt.

These days, late at night when my only companion was a flickering television, our love seemed like a blaze that had fizzled, leaving the ashes cold. But although she no longer called me Twinkle Butt, I was sure that if we sifted the ashes we could find a spark. I imagined what it would be like to fan the spark. Not into a wildfire—the days of wildfires were gone for us. But even the thought of a small flame lit my fantasy.

So when the occasion arose that I might accompany her, without the children, to a weekend gathering of teachers in Edmonton, I saw an opportunity for us to find that missing spark and rekindle our love. The convention had promise. It was being held in a first-class hotel. There was a welcoming cocktail party and a banquet with entertainment. She had an expense allowance, her time commitment was not great, and Edmonton has many attractions.

At first she was hesitant to take me. She was looking forward to a weekend of fun with her fellow teachers. When I explained that to celebrate the trip, I planned on buying each of us a new wardrobe, she immediately saw logic in the quest.

I convinced her to cancel plans to drive to Edmonton with her best friend so that we might ride the Dayliner, a train that runs between the two cities. The journey was less than four hours and I thought it would begin healing the bruises on our relationship. Relaxing in the club car, watching the scenery, toasting each other with fancy drinks, and feasting in elegance in the dining car would be important first steps toward locating the missing spark. In a flash of romantic inspiration, I booked an expensive suite, which according to the hotel brochure was sure to inspire notions of romance.

As we drove to the station, my wife was singing—something I hadn't heard since the previous summer, when I had yanked a spacer from the deck I was constructing and stuck one end into my forehead.

Our train was late. Her shoulders became stiff and she studied a crossword puzzle for the next two hours. The train, when it arrived, consisted of only one car, which was reasonable because we were the only passengers.

I stowed my suitcase on the luggage rack but left hers at the end of the car because it was too large to lift. She is a good planner and thinks of every contingency, even packing sheets, blankets, and pillows in case the hotel is too poor to afford its own.

When we sat, clouds of dust sprang up from the seats and remained suspended around us, each speck visible in the afternoon sun shining through the dirty windows. The wife held a handkerchief to her face but it didn't prevent a fit of choking.

She was still coughing when a man in oily coveralls walked through the car.

"Where can we get a drink and when do we eat?" I asked.

He looked at me as though I were unable to tie my own shoelaces. Then he laughed.

"This is a short trip," he said. "There is no dining car, no food, and no drinks." He walked away chuckling.

My wife's shoulders stiffened again and she made her mouth into a hyphen. Staring at me, she tore the crossword puzzle into tiny pieces. In this fashion we passed the time of the trip, which was longer than four hours because we stopped to enjoy the unparalleled views of Main Street in every town between Calgary and Edmonton. I rubbed a small hole in the dirt on the window to watch the passing scenery. It took my mind off the crossword puzzle.

When the sun went down, I saw the city lights. We came to a stop and the man in coveralls reappeared. "End of the line, folks. You get off here," he said.

"But we're not downtown," I answered.

"We don't go downtown. We're in the rail yard at the edge of the city," he explained.

I carried the bags. Everything was locked and dark. There was no taxi. The phone booth sported an Out of Order sign. We trudged along a dirt road while the wife spoke encouragement by spelling out my fate should I damage her suitcase.

When we came to a residential neighborhood, I approached a house, knocked on the door, and asked the lady who answered if I could use her phone. She slammed the door in my face.

After an hour we found a corner store and called a cab, which worked its way through Friday evening traffic and deposited us at our hotel. I dragged the suitcases to the front desk. The clerk smiled at me.

"You're hours late," he said. "Your room wasn't confirmed. We gave it away a long time ago."

"Then give me another room," I said.

"We're filled with teachers. I'm sorry, but there's nothing available." He smiled again, which made him appear not as sorry as he claimed to feel.

My wife's heels clicked as she marched back and forth in the center of the lobby.

I handed the clerk a twenty. "You have to find a room," I said. "It's worth my life."

He pocketed the twenty. "There is a conference room," he said. "We can roll cots in. It has a basin and toilet but no bath. You'll have to be out before eight. There's a meeting in the morning."

I glanced at my wife, pacing like a bear in a cage. It was probably the light, but it looked like steam was rising from the back of her neck.

"We'll take it," I said.

We rode the elevator. The bellhop opened the door, dropped our suitcases, and held out his hand.

"What the hell?" My wife exploded. Normally she doesn't use foul language, but she will make an exception. The bellhop looked at her face and ran.

"They gave away our room," I explained. "This is all that's left."

"The cold weather has frozen your brain. I'm not sleeping here." She marched into the bathroom.

There was a phone on a table in the corner. My sixth call was successful—a Holiday Inn on the other side of the city had a room. I shouted the news. After a wait, during which I thought I heard glass breaking, she emerged and paraded out the door. I grabbed the suitcases and followed. We hailed a cab, and an hour later we were in our new room.

The temperature of our relationship rose a few degrees. I relaxed. The cocktail party at our original hotel beckoned; drinks and snacks were exactly what we needed before a late romantic dinner. We returned to the hotel.

The ballroom was quiet. A man swept the floor. Two ladies gathered glasses and stacked chairs.

"Excuse me. Isn't this where the teacher's party is supposed to be?" I asked.

"Yes," the man answered. "But it's over. Everyone's gone."

There was nothing for it but to return to the Holiday Inn, where my wife again went into the bathroom. I called room service and ordered a bottle of champagne and a late dinner. She came out and I went in to wash. When I returned, she was in bed with her back to me.

I started to take off my clothes. I hadn't realized it would be this easy to recover the spark.

"Dinner is on its way," I said. "Let's share an appetizer before it gets here."

She didn't answer.

"They're bringing champagne." I lifted the blanket and prepared to slide into bed.

She spoke to the wall. "Take your champagne and sleep in the bathtub."

There was a knock on the door. I kept the champagne and sent the dinners back. Then I found a blanket and tried to get comfortable in the tub. I sipped the bubbly and shifted from one side to the other. The tub made my back and neck sore. Sleep was impossible. I started to feel that perhaps the spark *was* dead. The more I drank, the more I despaired. Finally, with my back so sore I could hardly get out of the tub, I decided to go for a walk.

The bar beside the lobby was open. Why not? If I could dull the pain, I might be able to sleep. I went in and ordered a double whiskey.

The drink burned all the way down. I ordered another and looked around. There were two other men at the bar. One was tall and had a black moustache. "Drowning your sorrows?" he asked.

"Yes, I am," I replied. "My wife told me I had to sleep in a bathtub."

The man laughed. "Sounds serious," he said. "My wife hasn't slept with me for five years. I understand how you feel. Let me buy you a drink."

"Me too," his friend said. "My wife doesn't talk to me."

Two more doubles arrived. They tasted wonderful. Everything was wonderful and the world was marvelous. I forgot about the bathtub and bought more whiskey, then a round of vodka to return the generosity of these newfound friends. Later, we drank brandy and smoked cigars while I related the tale of our train ride.

"You should have hitchhiked," Black Moustache said.

I found the idea incredibly funny and laughed until tears ran down my cheeks. My companions floated in and out of my vision, astounding me with their fabulous conversation. I was on the edge of great things, but felt completely tranquil. My wife might be angry, but these men understood. I drank some more.

Then something happened. My euphoria collapsed. I remembered my wife, alone upstairs, and my happiness turned to guilt. My new friends sympathized. Yes, the world was unjust. Yes, marriage was fraught with danger. Yes, we were unlucky in love.

After that, the evening became murky. I remember feeling ill and going to the bathroom. I also recall riding in a car.

I came to myself laying in a booth in a café. Someone was shaking me. There were plates and cups on the table.

"Wake up," a woman's voice said. "Your friends have gone. They said you'd pay."

Warm sun shone through the window. My hair hurt and my teeth itched. A hundred tiny devils pushed my brain against the backs of my eyes. "Where am I?" I asked.

"Right where your friends left you," she answered.

"I have to get back to the Holiday Inn. How far is it?"

She laughed. "You're nowhere near."

Somewhere in the depths of my hangover, a light bulb went on. I felt my pocket. Thank God—my wallet was still there. So was my room key.

"They said you'd pay," the waitress repeated.

The bill took every cent I had.

I went outside and began walking. I dreaded going back. I'd never been in so much trouble. I loved her and didn't relish the idea of spending the rest of my life alone. There was no doubt she would order me to leave. She'd probably already returned home to throw out my belongings and tell her friends about my treachery.

It was midmorning and my feet were sore by the time I entered the hotel. Perhaps she hadn't left. Maybe she was in the room waiting to kill me. I had no excuse and no speech ready. I turned the key and opened the door.

The curtains were closed and the only light came from a desk lamp. My wife was sitting in the shadows on the side of the bed. She looked up and I saw she was crying.

"Twinkle Butt," she whispered. Then she stood, ran across the room and threw her arms around me.

My mouth fell open. I had expected a flying water tumbler. The words poured from her. "You scared me half to death. I thought you'd gone. Please don't frighten me like that. I'll never be mean to you again." She shivered and sobbed, making my shirt wet.

I couldn't believe it. She thought I'd walked out because I was angry and left everything: her, my children, my home, my job. A lump formed in my throat. I opened my mouth to tell her the truth—that I'd gotten drunk and spent all my money.

"Don't cry," I said. "It's not like that. I didn't leave you. I … I …"

I opened my mouth but something made me stop: those years together, our children, her belief that I could actually take off like the good guy at the end of a cowboy movie. A tear rolled down my cheek. She'd called me Twinkle Butt, after all these years. Maybe it was better if she thought I was angry instead of stupid.

I pulled her close. "I won't leave again," I said.

She stretched up and kissed me. "I love you, Twinkle Butt," she said.

We held hands as we walked down for breakfast. I was tired and I had a hangover, but life was good.

Oh yes, and that spark? It became a wildfire!

Neil McKinnon and his wife Judy just celebrated their 45th wedding anniversary. Despite advancing years, he still occasionally gets called Twinkle Butt. A fictionalized version of Pains, Trains and Wildfires *appeared in* Tuckahoe Slidebottle *(Thistledown Press, 2006) which was shortlisted for the Stephen Leacock Humour Award and the Alberta Award for Short Fiction.*

A Fish Story

The one that almost got away.

By Doug Underhill

Serious fishermen all have stories about great battles with fighting fish, but there are few who have ever battled as long and hard as Donnie Grant of Canada's Maritimes when he landed a prized grilse in the summer of 1993. For those not in the know, a grilse is a young Atlantic salmon on its first return from the sea to fresh water.

Grant spends a good deal of the spring, summer, and fall angling the waters of the Miramichi River in New Brunswick, particularly the Main Southwest Miramichi. He also serves as a guide for non-resident anglers. Grant particularly likes to fish in the Howards area just above Blackville, which is where he caught this particular grilse.

The day was not a pleasant one weather-wise. "It was a terrible day," Grant told me. "It was overcast and miserable. But my wife had just bought me a new rod-holder for my canoe and I wanted to give it a try. I had a Coleman canoe with a lip on the gunwale, which meant the holder fit awkwardly." Nevertheless, Grant managed to secure it adequately using a wooden flange. He then got into the canoe and paddled out to where he wanted to fish.

Grant began casting with his new fishing outfit and it wasn't long before he hooked a grilse. He played the fish patiently until it settled down, and then he placed his rod in the new rod-holder and began poling for shore.

Once Grant started moving, to his utter disbelief, the grilse gave a final mighty jerk and pulled the rod loose from the holder. Grant watched helplessly as his rod, reel, line, and fish disappeared into ten feet of murky water. Not only had he lost all of his rigging, but he knew that it would be difficult explaining to his wife Fern that he had lost the fishing equipment she had just bought for him.

Grant spent some time trolling up and down the river, scanning the water for his lost gear. There was nothing. He finally gave up and forlornly poled his canoe back to camp. He tried to get some rest, but his mind was fixed firmly on his lost fishing equipment.

That night he came up with an idea. It was a long shot, but it was the only idea he had. He reasoned that the grilse would keep swimming and would eventually break free from the rod by snapping the leader, which was only six-pound test line. He then hypothesized that the line—which was a floating line—would rise to the surface of the water. And if he was lucky enough to find the floating line, he could pull his rod and reel back to the surface.

The next day was sunny and bright, and the water had cleared substantially. Grant paddled out to the general vicinity of the spot where he had lost everything. He moved back and forth across the river, then changed directions and moved up and down with the current. After what seemed a short eternity, he spotted something shiny glinting at the bottom of the riverbed. He recognized it immediately: his new J.R. Young reel.

Being a proactive kind of guy, Grant had brought with him a coat hanger and some duct tape. Attaching the coat hanger to the end of his paddle, he began dragging it through the water until he managed to hook the line with it. However, as he pulled it up he could feel tension on both ends, which probably meant it was caught on something.

When Grant finally got the rod and reel inside his canoe, he started to reel in the line. Then, seventy feet away, the grilse gave a tug and the fight was on again!

A banker from Nova Scotia happened to be sitting on the nearby shore. He had been watching Grant since the previous day and only now figured out what had happened. He offered to come out in his canoe and land it for Grant—an offer that Grant gladly accepted. This particular grilse would become a legend, and he didn't want it to get away.

Eventually the two men landed the grilse. And when they did, Grant not only had his special fish—and his fishing equipment back—but he also had the fishing story of a lifetime!

Doug Underhill of Miramichi, New Brunswick, is a retired English teacher and a professional writer and columnist. His eleven books include three poetry collections, three children's books, a humorous Miramichi Dictionary, a sports book (Baseball & Softball), two folklore/local history books, and Miramichi Fishing

Stories: All True of Course (Neptune Publishing Ltd. of St. John, New Brunswick) *from which this story was adapted. Underhill writes an online weekly fishing column and has been known to cast a few lines on both water and paper! Check out his website* **www.dougunderhill.com** *for more information about the man and the myth.*

Outside Looking In

When a vacation in Mexico turns into an episode of Survivor.

By Beth Deazeley

A week after meeting my new mother-in-law for the first time, I wound up wandering the back roads of Mexico in my pajamas.

My husband and I were married several weeks earlier, and for our honeymoon we had gone to break the news to his mother, who lives in a small town several hours outside Mexico City. On this particular day my husband and mother-in-law had gone into the city, and had left me alone in her house.

It was still early when I stepped out to check the weather. I was stretching in the doorway and enjoying the morning sunshine when I heard the door click shut and lock behind me.

I reeled off a string of curses in both English and Spanish. My Spanish wasn't great, but when it came to swearing, I could translate for the UN.

I sat down on the doorstep to consider my situation, resisting the urge to hyperventilate or cry. My husband and his mother wouldn't be home until late that evening. The house was surrounded by a run-down half-acre of avocado trees and bougainvillea enclosed by a high wall. The nearest neighbor was at least a kilometer away.

I thought about spending the day in the garden. The temperature was about fifteen degrees, but I knew it would reach thirty-five by noon. I also knew that it would likely pour rain for an hour in the afternoon. The trees provided little shelter. There was no water and the only available food were the unripe avocados in the trees.

And did I mention that I was barefoot and wearing pajamas? Suddenly the garden, formerly the site of huge family barbecues and tequila-fueled sing-alongs, had become a set for *Survivor.*

Spending the day in the garden would be distinctly uncomfortable. Moreover, my husband—who was sometimes frustrated by my seeming inability to fit in better within his country—would not be amused to arrive home in the evening to find his sunburned, soaked and starving wife staring wildly through the bars of the front gate. I couldn't even imagine what my mother-in-law would think. A good Mexican woman would never get locked out of her own house. This was just another strange misadventure that could only happen to a *gringa*.

Pressing my nose to the front window, I saw the house keys hanging on their hook below the statue of the *Virgen de Guadalupe*. I sent pleading thoughts in her direction, hoping for a miracle, but she just stared back at me, cold and smug. I gave her the finger and went exploring.

Iron bars protected each window. I remembered reading that if your head fits through an opening, the rest of the body can follow, so I spent several minutes trying unsuccessfully to jam my head between the bars of the living room window.

The kitchen door was also locked. Peering in, I spied a bottle on the counter and, for the first time in my life, craved tequila before lunch.

I suddenly remembered that there was one more door: one that led to the interior patio, which housed the boiler and the ancient stone sink where the cleaning lady washed the clothes. With a surge of hope, I remembered that the patio door didn't close properly. If my husband had fired up the boiler to heat water for his shower that morning, the door would still be open.

The patio was enclosed on all four sides by the house, so the only way I could reach it was via the roof. I scanned the weedy yard, searching for a ladder, and eventually found it by tripping over it. It was lying flat in the long grass, and suddenly so was I. More curses, directed vaguely at the ladder and at my husband for leaving me alone.

I hauled myself up, wrestled the ladder free from the weeds, and dragged it to the side of the house. The ladder looked ancient and was held precariously together by uneven slats and rusty nails. It creaked ominously when I stepped onto the first rung, but it bore my weight. I was grateful the house was only one story high.

The descent to the patio was easy; I lowered myself from the roof until I was standing in the stone sink. My big toe was turning blue and now one of my arms sported a long scrape, all courtesy of the ladder. With a sinking heart, I saw that the patio door was closed and locked. Apparently my macho husband had showered in cold water that morning. The house was locked on all sides.

As I clawed my way back up to the roof, I began shaking slightly. Trying to suppress my growing panic, I looked out into the distance, over the patchwork of farmland, the blue agave fields, and the rolling sierra. Not far off were the red roofs and white walls of the town where Consuela, the cleaning lady, lived. Then it stuck me: Consuela must have keys to the house!

I leapt to my feet and danced for joy. All I had to do was to climb over the garden wall, walk two kilometers in bare feet to Consuela's house, communicate my problem using basic Spanish and sign language, and presto … keys!

I half-climbed, half-fell down the ladder and trotted purposefully to the garden wall. It was twelve feet high with a locked gate, but nothing was going to stop me now. Using the bars of the gate and a nearby garbage can, I clawed my way up the wall and hauled myself over the top.

Then, as I scrabbled for a handhold on the far side, disaster struck. I saw the creature at the last second, but it was too late. My fingers had already reached into the crevice where the scorpion was sunning itself. By the time my brain registered the scuttling black shape with its pincer arms and arched tail, the sting was already burning up my arm. I lost my grip on the wall and fell into a pile of leaves and garbage bags outside the gate.

For the first three minutes I did the only thing one can do after being stung by a scorpion: roll around on the ground and moan. The sting of a scorpion in that part of Mexico isn't lethal, but it is painful. I eventually staggered to my feet, brushed off the worst of the leaf mold, and set off unsteadily down the dirt road into town.

The dust on the road was ankle-deep. In bare feet, with the sun beating down, it felt almost like walking on a beach. I passed cornfields, lime orchards, and empty lots filled with rubble and garbage. A parade of cars, trucks, horses, and burros passed, but no one spoke to me. My husband and I were regarded with suspicion. We were recent arrivals from the city, and we didn't attend the local church. Worst of all, I was a foreigner: a blonde-haired *gringa*. I could only imagine what they thought of me with my hair full of weeds, limping barefoot down the road wearing torn and filthy pajamas. I alternated between trying to stay invisible and trying to act like everything was normal.

Suddenly, ferocious barking erupted to my right. I shrieked. A Rottweiler, black as sin, was sprinting across the field towards me. I tried desperately to remember what my husband had told me about Mexican guard dogs.

It won't touch you if you're on the road. It was charging like a freight train.

It's only trained to protect the property. It was getting closer and closer.

It won't set foot on the road. It was *on* the road!

Help! No fair! That was against the rules!

Then I remembered: I needed a rock! Even pretending to throw a rock will scare off most dogs.

As my eyes locked on the salivating jaws, I scrabbled blindly in the dust with my one uninjured hand. Guadalupe had not completely abandoned me—my hand closed on a smooth, heavy rock with a sharp end. I raised it high and the dog skidded to a halt, wheeled, and ran back the way it had come.

I kissed my rock and deposited it in the pocket of my pajamas. The weight threatened to pull the flimsy pants off my hip, but there was no way I was going to leave it behind.

I stumbled through town, trying harder than ever to become invisible. As always, a group of children appeared out of nowhere and began following me. At first they kept a cautious distance, but after a while they sidled closer, pointing and laughing as they did. At least my lack of footwear didn't strike them as odd, since there was barely a pair of grubby tennis shoes among them.

As I passed through the center of town, everyone stopped what they were doing to stare at me: stone-faced old men, gossiping señoras, smirking young men. Dozens of unblinking black eyes followed me. I gritted my teeth against the throbbing in my hand and whistled to myself, trying to give the impression that we did this every day where I came from.

I was incredibly relieved to reach Consuela's cement blockhouse.

I approached the door, stepping over a crawling baby and dodging a vicious-looking rooster. I knocked on the open door and a girl of about five appeared. She screamed and ran away. I knocked again. A larger version of the first girl appeared and regarded me silently. I recalled that Consuela had sixteen children.

"Consuela?" I asked hopefully. The girl vanished. I waited, my arm twitching involuntarily. I was starting to feel sick. The rooster made another pass and was backing me into a corner when Consuela appeared. She looked me up and down and pulled me inside, ushering me into a living room that held little furniture but was packed with doilies, rosaries, and paintings of religious figures with large spiky halos.

I opened my mouth and realized that I didn't have the slightest idea how to explain what had happened. I shuffled, twisted my hands in my pockets, and found my rock, which I placed carefully on the coffee table as I searched for the Spanish words.

"The ... umm ... *puerta*..." The door. Good start.

I clapped my hands together in imitation of a door slamming shut.

"And ... *yo* ... *afuera* ... locked out."

Consuela must have thought I was an idiot. She would never have believed that in my own language I was reasonably articulate. Back home I had a real job for which I wore a suit and people were polite to me and I never, ever, wandered the streets in my pajamas.

Finally I remembered the word for keys. Giving Consuela my most charming smile, I asked, "*Las llaves?*"

She disappeared, then returned a minute later with the keys to the house. I jumped to my feet, trying to grab them from her hand without looking like I was grabbing them from her hand. I wanted to hug her, but I was too dirty.

"*Gracias! Gracias!*" I babbled.

I scooped up my rock and was halfway out the door when she stopped me. She pointed to my bare, filthy feet. Another long story; I shook my head. She motioned for me to wait and stepped into the dimness of the hall, reappearing with a pair of plastic sandals. I smiled my thanks and attempted to slip one on, only to discover that the sandal was half the size of my foot.

I shrugged awkwardly, looking at Consuela's tiny Mexican feet and feeling like a giant, duck-footed freak. She scooped up the shoes, motioned for me to wait again, and came back with another pair, which apparently belonged to her husband.

So with my toes hanging out of her husband's sandals, I began my homeward journey, clutching my precious keys. Emboldened by my footwear, I took a kick at the rooster on my way past.

I marched defiantly back through town. I had sandals, I had keys, and despite my bumps, scrapes, and scorpion sting, I had triumphed! I stared down the local busybodies. As I left the village, the Rottweiler made its snarling approach, but I was ready, rock in hand, and he didn't dare set foot off his property.

I was almost home when a pickup truck came thundering up the empty road behind me, the music of *Los Tigres del Norte* blasting on the stereo. The truck slowed and its occupants began chanting a chorus of "Hey, baby!" I ignored them, and after pacing me for an endless minute, the truck turned around and roared off the way it had come.

The bottom dropped out of my stomach when I heard the roar and the music approaching from behind me once again. They had come around for another pass. Even if I ran, I wouldn't make it to our gate in time.

I glanced out of the corner of my eye. There were three of them, drinking beer from oversize bottles. They pulled up beside me. I refused to look. The truck suddenly pulled in front of me, blocking my path. It stopped. Feet clad in cowboy boots stepped onto the road.

That was the last straw. Something snapped inside me and suddenly I was red-faced and shouting and stomping my sandals in the dust, yelling about doors and ladders and scorpions and waving my pointy rock. A wild gesture caused the rock to slip from my sweaty fingers and I watched as it arced gracefully through the air and shattered the back window of the truck.

Cursing crazy foreign women, the men departed in a cloud of dust. I leaned over and vomited at the side of the road, trying not to spatter my borrowed sandals.

Ten minutes later I was home. I unlocked the front door and fell to my knees inside. The door clicked shut softly behind me. Ignoring the disapproving stare of the Virgen de Guadalupe, I crawled directly to the tequila bottle.

Beth Deazeley is a recovering lawyer and is such an enthusiastic Spanish student that she married her teacher. She is a constant source of puzzlement to her in-laws.

Tarred and Feathered

Just when you thought it was safe to go back on the water.

By John Orlowski

In the town of Cape Elizabeth, there is a natural formation that the locals use as a launching ramp for all types of watercraft. It consists of two twenty-meter granite spits situated about ten meters apart, protecting between them a natural boat ramp that allows boat enthusiasts to drop a canoe, kayak, or powerboat. This ramp dumps you out into the northernmost part of Saco Bay, an area called Kettle Cove, which is sheltered by a sizable island and forms a lovely and protected playground and feeding area for the local seal population.

About seven years ago, shortly after separating from my wife, I decided to go for a quiet Sunday morning paddle in my kayak. It was Father's Day and I wanted to do something just for me.

I put in fairly early, wanting to be alone on the water. On a scale of one to ten, I would have given the conditions an eleven. Above me was a cobalt sky scattered with occasional cotton balls of cumulus, held motionless for what seemed like decorative purpose. The water was mirror smooth.

I paddled out several hundred meters to the center of the cove, hoping to enjoy some solitude before the powerboats started spoiling the scene with their noisy antics. It was the perfect picture of relaxation and exactly the kind of tonic I needed for my private Father's Day celebration.

After about an hour of bobbing gently in the bay and reading a Tom Clancy novel, something in the water caught my eye. A flash! Then another. Several more flashes!

"Cool!" I said out loud.

Fish surrounded my boat, their silver scales flashing like shards of aluminum as they pushed up toward the surface. I was enthralled. The sea was supplying me with personalized entertainment right beneath my boat.

As I continued to watch intently, the flashes became more frequent and pronounced in their intensity. The water around the boat started to roil and bubble with a seething mass of silver bodies. Fins and scales broke the surface, splashing me with seawater. It was rather refreshing in the heat of the morning, but also unsettling given that I was by myself a fair distance off shore.

As the splashing continued to intensify, fish started jumping right out of the water. It wasn't long before they were bouncing off the deck of my kayak, leaving scales and bloody streaks behind.

Then I realized what was happening: the fish I had been so delighted to see were maidenhead (also known as porgies) and they had been drawn to the white hull of my kayak. The large school had, in turn, drawn the attention of a school of bluefish, which were now feeding on the baitfish and making my situation less tenable and decidedly less serene.

Floating in a boat that was becoming increasingly smeared with scales, slime, and blood, I decided it was time to beat a hasty retreat. I dipped my paddle and stroked off at a rate reminiscent of the local kayak racers, determined to outrun the situation.

I made it all the way to shore, stopping for a breather only when I was few meters from the boat ramp. At this point there was only about a meter and a half of seawater under my boat.

Little did I know the school of maidenheads had followed my kayak all the way into the shallows, bringing the predators with them in hot pursuit. Things degenerated further. My kayak, slathered with fish innards, was suddenly in the middle of a virtual washing machine of agitated water.

It didn't take long for the commotion to draw the attention of several dozen aggressive seagulls. Not predisposed to giving up an easy meal, the gulls began dive-bombing the school of fish, all within a paddle's length of my boat. Guts, blood, slime, and feathers swirled everywhere. Seagull poop fell from the sky. I was completely overwhelmed.

Yuck!

Adrenaline pumping, my face covered with muck, I paddled hard for the boat ramp, gliding into it with a heavy thud. The maidenheads, running out of depth, left abruptly, taking the predators with them. Once again, the water around me was calm.

Whew! That was nasty. Virtually tarred and feathered.

It was then that I looked up from my boat to the twin granite spits that towered on either side. Looking down at me was a group of about fifty people, their mouths agape at what they had just witnessed. A few seconds later, they broke into loud applause, cheers, and uproarious laughter.

What else could I do? I climbed from my kayak, gave a deep bow, and then jumped into the ocean to clean off.

Chagrin was my lot that day. But at least I avoided a direct hit from the seagull poop. Awfully nice of those birdbrains to spare me that on Father's Day.

John Orlowski indulges himself in several outdoor hobbies, has varied interests in natural sciences, and has had experience in a diverse range of careers and subsequent retirements. However, he is not a fisherman, nor does he care to study or be intimately acquainted with carnivorous avians.

Kansas City Charades

When you're left high and dry in the Kansas City airport.

By Dorothea Helms

You can criticize television all you like, but I'm living proof that watching TV comedy shows is a practical thing to do. For a few minutes in the Kansas City International Airport, I was Lucille Ball, Mary Tyler Moore, and Carol Burnett all rolled into one.

It happened about a decade ago, when I was traveling to Broken Bow, Nebraska, to attend a Humor Writing Conference—and trust me, the people there are downright funny. They have to be to survive in a town called Broken Bow, where at that time you could buy gift items and guns in the same quaint shop.

In any case, my trip involved four legs: Toronto to Philadelphia, Philadelphia to Kansas City, Kansas City to Omaha, and finally, a five-hour van ride to the western equivalent of Mayberry. The first two flights out of the busy Toronto and Philly airports were uneventful but hectic, and I was relieved when I finally entered the Kansas City airport. Where the Philadelphia facility was crowded and dingy, with the aroma of overdone hot dogs wafting through a haze of stale cigarette smoke, I found walking into the Kansas

City building akin to sliding into a brand-new full-size car. It was bright, clean, and spacious, and I swear it smelled like polished fine leather.

As I searched for my gate, I strolled along curving corridors devoid of screaming children and harried flight attendants scurrying to make their connecting flights. Puzzled by, and somewhat suspicious at the dearth of people in this attractive facility, I rationalized that I'd never been to Kansas City before, and maybe everyone was standing on the corner of 12th Street and Vine picking up crazy little women.

I approached the correct gate and completed a lightning-fast scan of the area. Lo and behold, I was the only person there. I concentrated on studying the schedule board to determine whether my next flight would leave on time. Having checked my large suitcase, all I was carrying was a small red bag, which I set down on the floor next to one of the fifty or so plastic seats arranged around the gate desk.

I made a mental note that I had at least half an hour to wait before the airline would begin boarding passengers. Then, in one graceful motion and without really paying attention to where I was sitting down, I swung myself onto one of the numerous empty chairs.

The next few seconds took on an eerie, slow-motion kind of ambience as I realized I'd sat on a seat covered with liquid.

The squishing sound, followed by a cold wetness that immediately permeated my navy slacks and panties, prompted my eyes and mouth to open as wide as Lucy Ricardo's did when she realized she'd thrown a pie in William Holden's face. I felt mortified, just like Mary Tyler Moore must have when Lou Grant helped himself to three people's portions of Veal St. Olaf she had served at her dinner party. What to do … what to do … what to do? In thirty minutes or so I had to board a plane for Omaha—and I had no extra clothes to change into.

I sidled awkwardly into the nearby ladies' room to surmise the extent of the damage, hiding my posterior from a non-existent audience. The Kansas City International Airport had had the foresight to install a full-length mirror in there, and I cringed as I backed up and looked over my shoulder to take in the view. There's no delicate way of putting it—it looked as though I'd wet my pants. At least the liquid in question seemed to be water, and not something vile such as sticky orange juice or soured baby formula.

In true Carol Burnett style, I devised a plan. Usually I curse restrooms that have those air hand dryers instead of good old paper towels, but I was relieved that this one was equipped with an electric air blower secured to the wall just above the height of my waist. I found that if I backed up to within a few inches of the dryer, it blew air onto my bottom. Twenty minutes of this, I figured, and I'd be back to normal.

What I didn't count on in this until-now "empty" airport was other women coming in to use the restroom.

When I heard the click of high heels on the tiled entryway, I panicked, whirled around to face a sink, and proceeded to wash my hands, acting as innocent as I could. As soon as the perfectly coiffed businesswoman was ensconced in a stall, I whipped around and realigned my butt with the warm air from the dryer.

It was inevitable that I heard a flush, and when I did, I spun around to wash my hands again, all the time wondering whether the elegant stranger had seen my wet pants or just assumed I had a bad case of obsessive-compulsive disorder. In what seemed like an interminable amount of time, she left.

As I backed up to the dryer again, I heard TWO sets of heels clicking on the ceramic floor. Drat the luck, I thought. (Okay, maybe I used language that was a little coarser than that.) Like an Olympic ice skater, I launched into a cleverly choreographed ballet of hand washing and butt drying that I synchronized with the bathroom visits of each woman.

When three more intruders invaded my sacred space, I added to my dance steps a component of pretending to brush lint off my jacket as I stood with my back to the mirror (mainly because my hands were shriveling up from the application of so much soap and water). And so it went: wash hands, dry bottom, brush fake lint, etcetera—all timed so that no woman outside a stall ever saw the bottom-drying portion. Carol Burnett couldn't have pulled it off any better in a comedy skit, even if Harvey Korman and Tim Conway had entered the ladies' room in drag.

I shoved out of my mind insecurities resulting from paranoia that the women gathering at my gate were whispering about the weirdo in the washroom, because my pants were in fact drying. By the time I emerged from the restroom into the bright airport lights, I resembled a typical traveler, and I acted as though nothing out of the ordinary had happened. I knew that it was just my imagination that several sets of eyes stole judgmental glances in my direction. Besides, I'd never see any of these people again, I assured myself.

What a coincidence it was that when I boarded the plane, I found myself seated next to Intruder Number One. And how fascinating the book she was reading must have been—she never looked up from it once in an attempt to get to know me better.

The rest of my trip was a success, and at the humor conference I learned a valuable lesson: there's nothing you can make up that's funnier than real life.

Dorothea Helms, a.k.a. The Writing Fairy®, spent her formative years watching TV sitcoms and thinking they would prepare her for real life – which they did! This successful freelancer lives in Sunderland, Ontario, teaches creative writing, and is the author of The Writing Fairy Guide to Calling Yourself a Writer. *She has travelled to exotic locales such as Paris, France and Broken Bow, Nebraska, and has managed to milk a money-generating article out of every trip.*

Crotch Brake

Ouch, ouch, ouch, ouch, ouch....

By Sarah Bonar

At the early age of six months, I became aware that my dad—a man living life to the fullest and fastest—was an accident looking for a place to happen. If you're wondering how a child at that tender age could become so aware, just ask my mother.

Before I was born, my parents built a beautiful home in rural British Columbia, not far from the logging town of Prince George. One challenging (yet somewhat redeeming) fact about where they lived was the ample snowfall. It was not unusual for the area to receive up to ten feet of snow in a single winter. To give you an idea of how much snow would accumulate, several times a season, my father would have to climb onto the roof of the garage and shovel it off to prevent the garage from collapsing.

Fortunately, the roof of our house was well designed for the climate, and the sloped top allowed the snow to simply slide off. By midwinter, there would be an eight-foot embankment of snow around the house that my brother and I would climb, bringing us eye level to our mom, who was standing inside. We would stand there begging and pleading to be let back indoors. This of course would happen, immediately after being kicked outdoors "to get the stink blown off us."

The drive to our house from Prince George included a long and steep hill. Even at the best of times, it was treacherous. Our parents stored sandbags in the trunks of both cars to give them better traction in the winter. Yet I was told that on occasion, no matter how much sand was used, the car "was just not going to make it up the hill." And on these memorable occasions, even when my mom was pregnant with me—and a good thirty pounds heavier than usual—my dad would tell her to sit in the trunk.

His theory was that adding more weight to the back tires would give the car better traction, allowing them to force their way up the steepest parts of the Big Hill. My mom would have objected, but as the old saying goes: desperate times call for desperate measures. Only now, having been pregnant myself, I can appreciate my mom's displeasure at having to sit in the cold trunk, feeling the wind and snow whip around her face as my dad took repeated runs at the steep inclines.

Maybe buying chains for the car would have been logical, but where was the thrill and challenge in that?

Six months after I was born, my dad, being the inclusive parent that he is, decided that it would be good for everyone to go cross-country skiing in the backcountry near our home. My mom, who begrudgingly goes along with most of his ideas, did have some trepidation when he suggested it.

I was bundled up and placed in a baby backpack on my father's back. The ski trip went along smoothly until they came to the first downhill slope. I can image my mom saying, "Oh Gerry, do you think this is a good idea?" She always says that when she has any doubt as to my dad's ideas (which is often). My dad, loving the thrill of danger and the excitement of speed, would naturally *have* to partake in any activity that she questioned. Adrenaline clouding his better judgment, he made the decision to ski down the slope with a six-month-old baby on his back.

As the story has been told to me several times, he peered down the slope, began his decent, let out his characteristic "Yeee haaaw!" and promptly lost control. The ski descent ended in a gigantic wipeout at the bottom of the hill. My mom said that my dad quickly collected himself, then reached over to the snow bank and yanked me out by my feet, which were the only parts of my body still visible. Apparently it only took that one wipeout for me to realize that being attached to my dad in any form could be dangerous; at the top of every hill, I could be heard whimpering before a decent with my father.

My dad is an avid outdoorsman and certainly enjoys his winter activities. I would be remiss if I didn't state that he has gone on many ski trips without incident, but it's his habit of pushing his skiing adventures to the maximum that tends to create the stories we love to tell. And retell.

One such incident happened a few years ago when my dad went skiing with my brother, Andrew, and a family friend, Ray Hamilton. It should be mentioned that Ray is an eighty-year-old man who looks not a day over sixty. His health and well-being can no doubt be credited to his decades of physical work, the support of his loving family and doting wife, and his level-headed approach to life; the mental *yin* to my father's *yang*, so to speak.

It was a beautiful winter day, the winter sun shining on a fresh dump of champagne powder. My father and brother were excited to hit the trails on the outskirts of town, and invited Ray to come along. My dad would spend countless hours in the preseason prepping his equipment: fixing gouges in the base of his hickory and lignostone skis, plus hours of waxing and polishing the bases to ensure everything was in working order. All of this prep time would serve to build anticipation and excitement for the coming season, and ultimately for the one day of truly epic conditions. This was that day.

The plan was to go out for a few hours and be home by lunch. As they were only going to ski for the morning, they only brought basic supplies: their skiing clothes and equipment. My dad was dismayed when they picked up Ray and saw that he had brought his backpack loaded with "a spare set of everything."

The day of skiing proved to be the epic day they had all hoped for. There was fluffy powder almost two feet deep, and they were the first ones making fresh tracks on the trails. There was also the beautiful scenery of the mountains and trees cloaked in sparkling white.

As they began to loop back and start their trek home, they came to a series of hills, some of which were quite steep. My dad offered the following piece of advice to both Ray and Andrew: "When you begin your descent, just put your poles between your legs and pull them back to slow yourself down." I think the maneuver may have come to my dad in a pre-season dream.

My brother, who was in his early twenties at the time and still concerned about how he looked and behaved in public, decided to go first, wisely opting to ignore my dad's advice. He began his descent, and even though there was fresh powder to slow him, he fell on the second slope. He had quite a lot of speed, so when he crashed, his gear was scattered across the slope. It took him a few minutes to collect himself so that the next skier could get by.

My dad, after witnessing the crash from the top of the long hill, became even more convinced that his idea would be his saving grace. He began his descent and immediately put both poles between his legs, pulling them back gently to slow himself down. Initially the maneuver seemed to work, but as the slope grew steeper—and because there were already tracks to ride—he began to pick up more speed than my brother had.

My brother says that from his vantage point he could see the look on my dad's face, which began as a "this is how the professionals do things" expression. As he began to pick up speed, that expression changed to one of panic and worry. But instead of changing tactics, he continued downhill with poles between his legs, reefing on them all the more in an attempt to slow his descent. He flew past my brother, letting loose with his trademark "Yeee haaw!" and producing a huge rooster tail of powdery snow as he disappeared over the crest of the next hill.

Ray began his descent next. After what he had witnessed, he also opted not to use my dad's braking technique. Instead he cruised down the steep hill slowly and in complete control. He met up with my brother and together they followed my dad's tracks. They found him about three-quarters of the way down the last hill.

My dad had fallen … and not gently. The massive wipeout had left his hat, sunglasses, poles, and other ski paraphernalia strewn across the mountain slope. Andrew helped my father as he struggled back to his feet, noticing as he did so that both of my father's ski pole straps were still around his wrists. One pole was badly bent, while the other had snapped in half.

"Are you okay, Dad?" Andrew asked.

"Yeah, I'm just a little sore." He could barely respond through the obvious pain. Trying to distract Andrew and Ray, he continued, "I can't believe these poles! They must be defective. I'll have to take them back and get a decent pair."

Ray, as I said, is the *yin* to my father's *yang*. He graciously pulled a telescoping pole from his gear-laden backpack and handed it to my father. This made the final ten-kilometer trek somewhat manageable.

My mom and I were lounging in the living room, reading our books and sipping tea with a cozy fire snapping away in the stone fireplace, when my dad and brother finally arrived home. They were later than we had expected, but we credited that to the beautiful skiing conditions. We also knew that Ray was with them, so they were in good hands and we were not worried.

My dad staggered in through the front door, soaking wet and limping badly. He mumbled something about pulling a groin muscle and told us he was going to lie down, leaving Andrew to unpack the car. It wasn't until my father was asleep that my brother dared tell us the story of dad's Nordic braking system.

To this day, we don't know if my dad ever returned the "defective" ski poles.

Sarah Bonar has been writing for a few years, and enjoys documenting the daily plights of both her father and her children. They have much in common: they take on the world with enthusiasm while seeking a thrill along the way. Sarah's story "Skiing with Dad" appeared in the Summit Studios anthology A Beaver is Eating My Canoe *(2008). She is now hopelessly smitten with the idea of writing tales to entertain. More of Sarah's stories can be found on her blog: **www.sbonar.wordpress.com**.*

Choose Your Own Adventure

Drowning in a river, getting eaten my mosquitoes …
there are just so many options.

By Steve Bramucci

Congratulations! You've just arrived in the bustling city of Tena, Ecuador after a long day of bus travel from Quito. This is the last major outpost before a hundred or so miles of jungle and then the Peruvian border. You have been dreaming of the Amazon jungle since you were a boy, and you are very excited to be here.

Walking down one of the main streets, you notice that the town hosts five different Adventure Travel Operators. As you investigate these options, you find that each tour looks to be interesting and perfectly pleasant. You:

(a) Sign up for one of these company-run tours.

(b) Decide to avoid the tour packages by renting a bike so you can find a secret lagoon recommended to you by a local. The lagoon is supposedly tucked alongside the Rio Anzu. Your only map is written on a bar napkin.

Interesting choice! You're definitely the adventurous type, aren't you? Using your wobbly Spanish skills, you learn that the lagoon you're looking for is about twenty miles from town on a road that goes slightly uphill. You get some sleep and begin your ride at eight the next morning with all your camping equipment strapped to your back.

Speaking of equipment, you bring:

(a) Insect repellent and extra batteries for your flashlight, because "an ounce of prevention is worth a pound of cure."

(b) Mark Twain's *The Adventures of Huckleberry Finn* because it is your favorite river-related book.

You brought the book?! Of course you did. After all, who needs insect repellent in the Amazon Basin?

As the ride begins, you pedal through Tena toward your intended destination. When the pavement gives way to rocks and mud, you check the napkin to confirm that you're heading in the right direction. You are. However, while marveling at just how heavy your backpack feels, you realize that a screw is protruding upward from the bicycle seat. It pokes directly into your most tender areas. You:

(a) Begin to curse the seat, the bike, and gravity, particularly the latter for increasing the force that pulls you into the screw's pointy tip.

(b) Notice an elderly woman gathering firewood. As you watch her mount the heavy basket onto her back—using a strap across her forehead for leverage—you decide that you never have the right to complain again. Ever.

Bravo! You were able to do both things simultaneously.

You continue riding and soon arrive at the place your napkin map shows as the beginning of a slight incline. You quickly realize that you have mistranslated the phrase "slight incline." The correct translation should have been "straight uphill for five miles."

Sweating profusely, you arrive at your destination by midafternoon. The lagoon actually exists! Furthermore, it is incredible: a translucent pool above a waterfall, followed by a series of cascades tumbling downriver. You:

(a) Camp near the lagoon for easy access to the water.

(b) Set camp a half-mile away on a patch of sand. It's surrounded by granite boulders on the banks of the Rio Anzu and seems more idyllic.

Hmmmm. It's certainly more work to walk that extra distance, but so be it. No one can deny that the spot you chose is everything you ever imagined a tropical rainforest to be. The jungle trickles right out onto the boulders, and the little pool of water next to your camp hosts thousands of tadpoles and baby frogs. In the distance, the clouds hang in the trees like long, twisted tendrils of smoke.

As if on cue, a brilliant blue butterfly the size of a dinner plate lands next to you—the first of many butterflies you will see here. Within minutes, the number of butterflies and moths that have landed on you during your lifetime jumps from one to about two dozen. As you make camp, the sun continues to beat down, and when you need a break you ride down a small set of rapids using a plastic jerry can as a flotation device.

When you start to gather firewood, you estimate that it's around four o'clock. You quickly discover that finding dry wood in the rain forest is not the world's easiest task. You resort to burning the blank pages and editorial notes from *Huck Finn* to dry a few fallen leaves. These giant leaves, once dry, make an excellent fuel, but the bigger twigs dry more slowly.

For a few moments, this exercise reminds you of starting fires during the early spring in your home state of Oregon. This makes you feel nostalgic. That feeling evaporates when a large hairy spider that looks capable of flooding your body with deadly venom crawls out of the wood you've just gathered. Suddenly it becomes all too clear that you are not in Oregon. For more than two hours you struggle to get a flame going while simultaneously avoiding creepy crawlies like this spider. By sunset you are cooking a can of lentils while roasting onions, garlic, potatoes, and carrots in the fire's hot coals.

As darkness settles, you try to keep yourself from feeling spooked. Your fire doesn't provide enough light to eat by, so you use your flashlight. The batteries burn out by the end of your meal, but in some ways this may be a blessing; the light was attracting sand flies and they were biting you *everywhere*, even managing to reach some of those hard-to-reach places that your bicycle seat had been poking.

You hear heavy thuds off in the jungle—and you realize that this is the sound of an approaching Amazon thunderstorm. You dive for your tent just as the rain begins falling in coin-sized drops that land with such force that it seems like they are being thrown towards earth. A flash of lightning illuminates the entire river for just a second before everything goes black again. Thunder crashes above you. You:

(a) Remember reading something about Amazon River tributaries being prone to flash flooding and move camp IMMEDIATELY.

(b) Keep the thought in mind, but bide your time by eating a Nestlé Crunch bar that you've wisely carried for just such emergencies.

Okay, you've decided to stay put. Every few minutes, you reach your hands blindly out of the tent to see how much that little tadpole pond has infringed on your ten-foot by six-foot spit of sand. You alternate between moments of panic and moments of relief, but your tent stays dry and in one place. You decide to write to the good folks at REI to thank them for the quality of the rain flies.

The storm booms along for hours. It is a long night, but you manage some fitful sleep. At first light, you poke your head out of the tent and are pleased to see that your camp hasn't been breached. However, it is still raining. Considering how little you slept, you decide to laze around in the tent for a while. You reason that it's been raining all night and that it can't keep up much longer. You are:

(a) Correct. The storm soon weakens.

(b) A fool. This is the rainforest … it's right there in the name! The rain continues steadily, with a few touches of far-off thunder splashed around for effect.

Finally, around noon by your best guess, the rain lets up enough to let you slink outside. It's only then that you realize just how shockingly, appallingly, mind-numbingly lucky you have been. The river has risen at least two feet, and up to four or five feet in some places. You were protected on all sides by those granite boulders and your campsite hasn't actually changed all that much.

Don't go patting yourself on the back just yet, Bear Grylls. Remember that you chose it because it was "idyllic," not because it was "well protected."

Either way, you're still in a predicament. The river's rise has left you marooned on an island—a small spit of sand protected by two boulders on the upriver sides. Everything else is underwater. At first glance it looks like getting off the island with your bike and backpack will be impossible. But you soon notice some eddies from the shoreline and go on a few exploratory swims to check the water's depth. Finally, you find a place where the river is shallow enough to stand. Barely.

You begin crossing between your camp and the shore. It takes three trips, carrying your gear over your head, with the water lapping at your armpits. Once that task is finished you trudge through mud a foot deep, through the jungle and over a rickety bridge that crosses the lagoon. The spot that was so peaceful yesterday is now raging with whitewater.

You stay there for the rest of the day. You even go swimming, tying a safety rope to a rock so that you can splash around in the lagoon without getting pulled over the falls.

As the shadows start to lengthen, you begin the bike ride back to Tena, racing to get there before darkness falls. Even though it felt like the entire trip to the lagoon was uphill, the return trip somehow seems to have plenty of uphill, too. Knowing that you have to make it back to town in time to catch a bus, and that if you fail to do so you'll miss your flight to Los Angeles, you ride as fast as your weary legs can manage.

But before leaving the rainforest you make one final stop. You stand briefly to take it all in. With butterflies dancing circles around you, tropical birds calling from somewhere in the distance, and the fog twisting through the treetops, you realize:

(a) There are places you will visit that will never live up to your boyhood expectations, but the rainforest is definitely not one of them.

(b) You will definitely come back here someday.

(c) Both of the above.

Steve Bramucci is a travel writer based in Laguna Beach, California. He writes for COAST, Trazzler, The Weather Channel, *and a variety of other magazines and websites. He recently won* Trazzler's *national Oasis Travel Writing Contest. "Choose your own Adventure" has been adapted from a story that originally appeared in* InTravel *magazine, where it won the 2009 Reader's Choice award. Steve continues to seek out the adventures he dreamed of as a boy.*

Nature's Call

An ode to outdoor bathroom rituals.

By Allan Hardin

For my circle of friends who enjoy the great outdoors, the terms *fishing*, *camping*, and *hiking* are just euphemisms for gathering in the southern Alberta foothills to drink and get rowdy without (for the most part) disturbing your neighbors.

Aside from the rare occasion when someone in the group might bring a trailer, we leave most of the amenities of urban life at home. We cook our meals on a propane stove or over an open campfire; we sleep in tents or in the back of SUVs; and unless we are staying in a campground where there are outhouses for our daily waste management, each of us has developed an individual practice for answering nature's call.

Some of us like to go for a leisurely morning stroll into the forest, where we can select a fallen log to hang our fanny over. We can do our business while sitting and listening to the chattering of squirrels, the squawking of jays, and the relaxing hum of mosquitoes as they hover about our eyes and ears—not to mention the melodic buzzing of deer flies as they lick their hoary lips in anticipation of the soon-to-be-exposed mass of human posterior flesh.

One friend in particular (let's call him John) had the most curious of rituals. Several years ago he was dating a girl who wasn't particularly fond of our sojourns into the wilds; but to please the newfound love of her life, she put up a brave front and came "fishing" with the gang.

She smiled and put on an air of bravado as she stumbled over loose gravel and boulders while wading through hip-deep, ice-cold water to get to the next trout-filled pool. She waited patiently while John selected a specific fly that he thought might work and tied it on her line. She pretended to listen intently as John showed her over and over and over again how to cast the fly into areas of the pool where he thought the fish might be lurking.

This brave soul ate John's burnt steaks and drank his cheap beer (that's another story), but the one thing she would *not* do is squat in the bush to answer nature's call.

To that end, John came up with a contraption that seemed to placate her somewhat. He took a five-gallon lard pail, complete with a thick wire handle, cut the bottom off, and then fixed a plastic toilet seat to the top with screws and duct tape.

When it was required for use, he would insert a large garbage bag inside the pail and secure it with four or five rotations of duct tape to avoid any unforeseen problems with the bag falling through the bottom of the pail from the weight of the contents. Whenever his girlfriend had to do her business, she would hike deep into the woods with her portable toilet, far from prying eyes. We were all given strict instructions not to mention the grizzly bears and mountain lions that might be in the area.

I am sorry to tell you, dear reader, that the relationship did not last. John never did share the details, but most of us concluded it had something to do with "conflicting interests."

John did, however, keep the portable potty, and he developed a daily routine using said apparatus. He would roll out of bed and stumble bleary-eyed to the communal cooking area, where he would then rummage around until he found his drinking cup. After examining the cup to ensure that no insect had fallen inside and drowned in the dregs of the previous day's brew, he would make his way to the fire, where the large pot of my wife's coffee sat.

No matter what time of day it was, Linda always had a pot brewing. Hmmm—perhaps *brewing* isn't the right word. Let's try *fermenting*. The formula for a three-day camping trip is to brew a pot of fresh coffee upon arrival, which then serves as the base of all coffee for the duration of the trip. It thus becomes a matter of adding water and a couple scoops of ground coffee to the mix. People can then indulge themselves by drinking the coffee straight (not recommended for the faint of heart) or adding various liqueurs to make it a little more palatable.

After a cup or two of Linda's magic elixir, John would proceed to his van, where he would grab a newspaper and his porta potty. On rainy days he would find the nearest spot that offered some shelter and do his business as quickly as possible, sans newspaper. But on sunny days John would scout around until he found an open spot with full exposure to the morning sun, after which he would find a level spot for the pail, drop his drawers, and sit. And unless we were in a hurry to go chase some trout, he would sit until he had read the entire paper.

On one occasion, we were camped about three kilometers from the main highway. We had gone up an old logging road that followed a creek to its headwaters and discovered an ideal camping spot: a small clearing between the logging road and the creek. It was a bright, sunny morning, and as per the previously described routine, John took his homemade porta potty and set it down on the road shoulder, despite protests from his new girlfriend that someone might come along and see him. John had already assumed his position and assured her that people seldom came up this road. And quite frankly, we all had to agree with him. We had not seen another person or vehicle for two days.

Isn't it funny how the minute you think you have things figured out, life says, "Oh, yeah," and throws you a curve ball? No sooner were the words out of John's mouth than two half-ton trucks full of people (in both the cabs and buckets) came wheeling around the corner.

The first truck stopped right beside John, and the driver leaned out the window and asked directions to another creek.

John never batted an eyelash. He lowered the paper, took his glasses off, pensively inserted one arm of his glasses into the corner of his mouth, and slowly shook his head back and forth. Then he carefully explained that they were on the wrong road, and that they should go back a short distance to where the road split and take the left fork.

The travelers continued a couple hundred yards further up the road, then took advantage of a wide section in the road to turn the vehicles around and head back the way they had come—but not without stopping beside John again to thank him.

John lowered his paper again and acknowledged their gratitude, nodding his head and replying, "No problem."

As the second truck passed, we noticed that one of the women in the back was taking pictures. No doubt John will be a source of great amusement every time this woman shows photographs of their camping trip to her friends and relatives.

Not to be outdone by a passing tourist, my wife Linda (unbeknownst to John) made her way through the willows to where she could get a good picture of John sitting on his throne. Upon our return to civilization, she ordered a glossy eight-by-ten print, which we framed and gave him for Christmas. We are not sure if John displays the picture or not, but he has vowed vengeance on Linda, which he has accomplished on several occasions.

But those are stories for another time.

*Allan lives in Calgary, Alberta where he writes western novels and gets even with his friends by submitting to publishers embarrassing anecdotes about their misadventures in the wilderness. You can find Allan in cyberspace at **www.allanhardinstoryteller.com**.*

Strange Bedfellows

What's that tingling sensation in my scalp?

By Mary Wellwood

I am a retired Ontario schoolteacher who several years ago, after becoming bored with retirement, decided to return to the classroom. I figured it would be an adventure to teach on a small Ojibwa First Nations reserve in northern Manitoba, so I applied for a job at the Poplar River reserve not far from Thompson.

For those not familiar with Manitoba, the reserve sits on the north shore of Lake Manitoba, more than six hundred kilometers due north of Winnipeg. It's surrounded on all sides by a vast and imposing wilderness. In the summer, the landscape is a jigsaw puzzle of lakes, trees, and rocks. In the winter, it becomes a jigsaw puzzle of *frozen* lakes, *frozen* trees, and *frozen* rocks.

Yes, it gets a wee bit cold up there. It can and often does drop to minus forty degrees Celsius—cold enough that local residents build ice roads and drive their vehicles across Lake Manitoba.

My teaching adventure required that I say goodbye to my family for an entire year. However, I could not bear to leave my little shih tzu Sensei behind. He and I are best buddies and we travel everywhere together. The school janitor in Poplar River built him a fenced-in compound at the back of my ground-level apartment so that the wild dogs that roam freely on the reserve wouldn't attack and kill him. He wouldn't have lasted long otherwise.

One particularly cold and snowy night, I was just getting ready for bed when a chorus of howling and angry barking penetrated into my little apartment. Sensei started to whimper, letting me know that somebody was in trouble outside. I tried to calm him down, but he wouldn't be appeased so easily. So I dressed in warm winter clothes, put on some gloves, and stepped outside into the raging blizzard.

I looked around and quickly spotted the subject of the dogs' attention: hiding in the corner of my front window alcove was a very scared little kitten. Wet and trembling violently, it looked utterly miserable. I grabbed it and brought it inside. As soon as I put it on the floor, however, it hissed loudly at Sensei, raised its hackles, and backed away. It was obvious that it wanted nothing to do with my dog.

The kitten was a funny-looking little thing with big feet, pointy ears, long whiskers, and a short stub of a tail. Most of its body was covered in brown spots. Despite its reaction to Sensei, the kitten seemed to like me and readily came into my arms to warm up. It curled up on my lap and fell asleep while I sat in my favorite chair and read a book.

I soon went to bed and brought the kitten into my room with me. It didn't mind in the slightest; it curled around the top of my head, purring loudly, and promptly went to sleep again. There it stayed for the entire night.

The next morning when I went to the school—which was just a few steps from my apartment—I asked if anybody had lost a kitten. They all gave me the same short answer: "We don't have cats on this reserve. The dogs would make short work of them."

I was puzzled. Where had this kitten come from?

I was leaving for a conference in Winnipeg on the afternoon flight and couldn't take the kitten with me, so I took her out to the porch, set her down, and said, "Now, sweetie, take your time going home. I'm sure mommy is waiting for you. Wait until you don't see any dogs, and then make a run for it."

I went back inside, and when I returned to the porch several minutes later she was gone. I shed a few tears, yet somehow I felt she was safe.

In Winnipeg, with a few hours to spare before the conference, I decided to spend some time in a nearby bookstore. As I browsed though the aisles, something grabbed my attention … a small postcard with a picture of a young lynx.

It looked exactly like the kitten that had slept in my bed the night before with its small furry body wrapped around my head.

Was my scalp tingling? No, not really. But I can honestly say that at that moment I felt a connection with nature I have never felt before.

Mary Wellwood's friends refer to her as "Grizzly Mary" because she loves teaching in remote northern communities. She lived in northern Manitoba for five years, and just last year taught at a school in a small First Nations community called Tsay Keh Dene in northern British Columbia. She is currently living with Sensei in London, Ontario, where he enjoys chasing squirrels in a nearby park.

Antler Girls

A Christmas road trip can be tonic for the soul.

By Lois Gordon

The road trip was one of those spur-of-the-moment ideas conceived during the euphoric afterglow that often accompanies an empty wine bottle. My friend Donna and I were looking for an escape from that most overrated time of year.

"Myrtle Beach for Christmas!"

"No obligatory family festivities!"

"Just a beach, some sun…"

"…a round or two of golf…"

"I'm there!" I declared with exuberance.

A week later we packed my station wagon with golf clubs, suitcases, a cooler full of food, and I-don't-know-how-many pairs of shoes. (In our defense, we were leaving snowy Ontario for temperate South Carolina. We would need boots for sure; walking shoes no doubt; golf shoes we hoped; sandals if there was a God; slippers for the hotel room; water shoes for the shower; and dancing shoes if we were supremely lucky. And an extra pair of most of these, because black is *not* a neutral color. I don't care what they say.)

"Mornin'," said the cheerless guard at U.S. Customs. "Where are you headed today?" He didn't sound like he cared much.

"Myrtle Beach," I said, wishing encounters with authority figures didn't leave me feeling like I was a fugitive from justice.

"For eight glorious days," Donna chirped from the passenger's side.

He peered into the back of the wagon, then regarded us over his bifocals. "What's in the cooler, ladies?"

"Oooooh!" Donna squealed, bouncing in her seat and flapping her hands like she was trying to put out a fire eight inches in front of her face. "We have smoked salmon—and all the accoutrements!" She started to drool. "And Brie and kiwis and grapes and Clamato, because we *have* to have a Caesar before lunch. And best of all, cham-*pagne!*"

I groaned. I was pretty sure we were in contravention of at least three laws that would send us straight back home—importing food, booze, and nut bars.

"We just have to stop at the Duty Free for some vodka and we're *all set!*" Donna added, batting her Doris Day eyes and endearing herself even to me.

The guard raised an eyebrow, grinned a half-smile, and said, "Have a nice trip, ladies."

"And the best part?" Donna called to him as I began closing the window. "We're playing golf on Christmas Day! *Wahoo!*"

"Good thing you're cute," I said, shaking my head, "or we'd be cooling our heels in Customs while they poured your Dom Pérignon down the sink."

There was only one impediment to what could have been a quick trip. Donna, it appeared, had an abiding fear of bridges.

"Ohmigosh, a bridge!" she exclaimed during her first turn behind the wheel.

"Uh-huh. Very good," I said. "And do you know what that is over there?" I pointed to a green barn.

She played along. "A *barn*. And that's a cow!"

"And this is the Susquehanna River," said I, consulting the map.

"And this would be the problem," Donna sang. "I don't do bridges."

"What do you mean, you don't do bridges?"

"I'm terrified of them," she said, pulling off onto the shoulder. "I can't drive over them. I panic."

"Just do what I do. Close your eyes."

"Seriously, I can't drive over that bridge. We're stuck here if you don't drive over it."

"You're kidding."

"No, I'm not kidding. If I have to drive over that thing, we'll die. I'm telling you … we'll *die!*"

"What would you do if I wasn't here to drive us over the bridge?"

"I'd turn around and go home," she said flatly.

"Okay," I sighed. "Trade places. I'll drive."

It was going to be a long trip—we were heading into the watery states of Maryland and Virginia. I swore that if I ever took another road trip with this lunatic, it would be to the Gobi freakin' Desert.

As we approached the river, I tried coaching my friend into accepting bridges for the valuable structures they are.

"Look at the view off to the left," I said in soothing tones. "Isn't that pretty? And to the right, see how the sun sparkles on the water? Beautiful! See? The bridge is our *friend*."

"Oh dear, oh dear, this isn't good," Donna moaned, covering her eyes.

"You just need a distraction. Let's sing!" I suggested, with the condescendingly sweet voice of an impatient babysitter. "Jingle bells, jingle bells…"

"Jingle all the way…" she joined in, her eyelids still squeezed shut.

"Oh what fun it is to ride…"

"Da da da da da!" Donna finished.

I stopped singing and stared at her.

She opened her eyes and stared back defiantly. "So, I don't know the words, okay?"

"You don't know the words to 'Jingle Bells'? *Everyone* knows the words to 'Jingle Bells.' Yasser Arafat knew the words to 'Jingle Bells'!"

"Well, I get them mixed up. I just know it ends with 'fa la la la la.'"

"No. That's 'Deck the Halls.'"

"Oh yeah! Deck the halls with boughs of holly," she trilled. "Fa la la la la, la la la la!" She looked so proud. It was like I had just watched my daughter tie her own shoes for the first time.

And we had made it over the bridge.

Her next turn at the wheel, though, was the same story. "I can't do this," she whimpered through clenched teeth.

"I'm right here beside you. We'll sing."

The bridge loomed. She tightened her grip on the wheel. "I don't know…"

"Oh, little town of Bethlehem…" I trilled.

"How still we see these ryes…"

"How still we see thee lie." I rolled my eyes. "Do you know *any* Christmas songs?"

"Well, there's that one about the three wise men," she offered hopefully.

"You mean 'We Three Kings'?"

"Yeah, that's it! 'We Three Kings Of Orientar.' I could never figure out where that was. Go ahead and try … you'll never find it on any map," she declared.

I wonder if my friend is one of those people who hovers between being brilliant and insane. It's a fine line, I'm told.

*   *   *

We rolled into Myrtle Beach and checked out the shopping district. In keeping with the spirit of the season, we purchased headbands sporting brown felt reindeer antlers. Donna's were festooned with a plaid ribbon and golden bells. Mine featured dangling Christmas tree lights. Donna looked adorable. I looked like Bullwinkle with breast implants.

We arrived at the hotel after dark, when the only view from our room was of faintly lit palm trees. Beyond lay a black ocean. We left the balcony door open and listened to the steady swish of waves. In the distance, a foghorn sounded faintly, turning the mood melancholy. However, the decorated miniature Christmas tree we had toted from Canada cheered us, and we toasted our success in arriving unscathed.

Hungry for dinner, we ventured down to the lobby, reindeer headbands in place, in search of the restaurant. After poking our heads into many doorways to find nothing but quiet darkness, we finally came across the bar.

The dim room was silent as a funeral home. Three couples drooped on bar stools; the bored bartender wiped glasses with a cloth. No one spoke. Donna and I looked at each other with raised eyebrows. Well, wasn't *this* just a jolly old place to be. I've seen friendlier faces inside the offices of Revenue Canada.

We edged forward. Eyes peered at us through the smoky haze as though we were apparitions materializing in the mist.

"Merry Christmas, everybody!" Donna said tentatively.

In one voice they answered, "Merry Christmas," sounding remarkably like the lighthouse foghorn.

"Hah," said the bartender. "Ah'm Buddy. What can ah get you ladies this evenin'?"

"Scotch," I said. I always drink Scotch at wakes.

"Where y'all from?" Buddy asked as he poured our drinks.

"Canada," we replied in unison.

"Ah thought so. When ah saw those antlers yure wearin' ah

thought, *those* girls must be from Canada."

We laughed. It was probably the first sound of joy that bar had heard in a long time.

"So, where are you all from?" Donna asked the barflies.

Linda and Don were from New Jersey. They were here because their kids had taken off to Florida for Christmas and they had no one else to share the holidays with.

Anne and Bill were from Philadelphia. Their kids hadn't invited them for the holidays, so they left town to assuage the hurt.

Rachelle and Bernie were here to play golf. They were in the bar because "every other goddam place in this godforsaken town was closed tonight."

These folks could suck the Christmas spirit out of a room faster than a Dyson vacuum cleaner.

Undaunted, Donna pressed on. "Know what? I've got my camera here, and I'd like to take your pictures. We're keeping a scrapbook of our trip, and you're all certainly part of the experience!"

"Wait!" said I. "They need antlers!"

They were too shocked to run screaming from the room. I popped the antlers onto their heads in turn.

"Now *smile!*" They stared into the flashing camera, their hangdog expressions caught on film for posterity.

But they smiled. Laughed, even. Long after our dinner had come and gone, we all sang Christmas songs at the top of our lungs. Donna, who couldn't keep the words straight, mimicked us half a beat behind, and that made everyone laugh louder.

"Whah, you antler girls are lahk a breath of fresh air." Buddy flashed a brilliant grin. "Ah was about ta slit ma wrists if you hadn'a come along."

When we finally staggered off our barstools, to a person they hugged us and offered a sincere "Merry Christmas!" They told us it had been some time since they'd laughed that much—and we believed them.

*   *   *

It was Christmas night in Myrtle Beach, and the hotel was putting on a show. Donna and I were particularly high-spirited; Buddy had sent a complimentary bottle of wine to our table because we dared to show up wearing our headbands. You don't need diamonds when you've got antlers.

The opening act was karaoke, which should, in my opinion, go back to Japan where it came from and leave us alone. Who really wants to find themselves at center stage, flipping back imaginary long hair and licking their upper teeth just like Cher does, because they're *cool* and a *really good* singer? Or is that just me?

The headliner, God bless him, tried his best. He crooned like Tom Jones as he wound his way through the half-empty cocktail lounge, caressing ladies under the chin, stroking their cheeks with his thumb, and making all our stomachs turn. No one would be tossing their panties at him that night.

Suddenly struck with empathy, Donna leapt to his rescue. She performed brilliantly, trading suggestive quips with the performer while she continued to sip from her champagne glass. The two of them finished off the set with a most provocative, outrageously funny *entre-deux* that culminated in a sexy tango. The audience roared with laughter and demanded an encore. The entertainer was left speechless.

The following night, the lounge was packed and there was a buzz of excitement in the air. Suddenly, a woman from Buffalo clutched Donna.

"What time do you go on, hon?" she asked.

"Go on what?" Donna frowned. Why was this stranger pushing an autograph book in her face?

"Why, on stage! What time is your performance? We met all these nice people at the golf course today and told them they *had* to come over and see the show!"

She pointed to a group seated at a nearby table.

"There they are! Couldja be a doll and just wave at them for me?" she gushed.

It's not often that Donna is at a loss for words. "I … I'm not part of the show."

"But *hon,* we just saw you last night!"

"Last night was, you know … impromptu."

"Oh, but *hon*! You were so *funny!* I was sure you were part of the show!" The woman harrumphed. "Well, *what* am I going to tell my friends? They all came to see you!"

Apparently, Donna has missed her calling.

With an ice storm threatening the eastern seaboard, Donna and I decided to head for home a day early. Besides, we had pretty much used up our repertoire of Christmas songs, and we had all those bridges to deal with.

Our American friends, including Buddy the bartender, showed up in the lobby to wish us farewell and a safe trip. Linda, who we had met on our first night in the bar, hugged both of us and whispered tearfully, "Thank you, Antler Girls."

Four simple words. And they meant the world to us.

Every Christmas Eve, I don those silly antlers and remember how I felt that night at that bar in Myrtle Beach. It's different now, of course. I could never recapture the same *joie de vivre*, but I smile when I think of that special Christmas spent in the company of strangers. As I grow older, I hope I never lose the irrepressible spirit of an Antler Girl.

Lois Gordon is a writer, shepherd, sailor, road warrior and interior designer. Humor is what sees her through rejection letters, bottle-fed lambs, fickle winds, flat tires and taupe, and in her spare time she hosts writers' retreats at her country home in southern Ontario. Lois won the Grand Prize in the 2010 Summit Studios contest for travel and outdoor humor writing. The antlers she purchased in South Carolina are still her favorite fashion accessory.

Duck!

I am Great White Hunter. Tremble in your feathers.

By Tim Billings

We drifted slowly down the alder-choked stream, occasionally having to grab branches to pull ourselves along. Fallen trees nearly blocked our way; someone had cut pieces out of them with a chainsaw, creating openings just wide enough for a canoe to slip through. This was prime swampland: the water was stained with tannin and choked with weeds. The bottom was a dark tangle of hundreds of years' worth of detritus—leaves and twigs—with sandbars scattered randomly about, places where we occasionally rested before digging our paddles into the murk to get moving again.

I had decided to try duck hunting with my college roommate Peter. We had tested our luck with partridges and snowshoe hares in the past, but this was the first time we'd ever set our sights on ducks. We packed up our canoe gear and shotguns and drove to Sunkaze stream in Old Town, Maine. Here was a giant marsh with water channels ribboned down its length, an area we thought would be perfect for duck hunting.

It was early November and it had been a very cold month. Pockets of the stream that saw little daylight already had a skim of ice covering them. The morning was calm and very cold, and as the sun began to rise, mist started steaming off the water. I was in the stern and Peter was in the bow. As we paddled through the many twists and turns, we tried to remember the route we were taking so that we could find our way back to the truck at the end of the day.

After some time Peter announced that he had to relieve himself. Seeing as how there wasn't any solid ground nearby, I nosed the canoe into a large hummock that was covered with grass and a few scraggly alders. As he stood up to take care of business, there was a sudden eruption of honking and flapping; a large flock of ducks had been hiding on the far side of the hummock. Once in the sky, they scattered in every direction. It seemed as though they were everywhere.

We sat in stunned silence. The ducks had been camouflaged to us until, by fate or dumb luck, we had picked that exact spot to use as a latrine. We started to scheme and quickly hatched a plan. We figured that with all the ducks flying around the marsh, it should be fairly easy to call one in.

We paddled downstream a short distance until we came to a wide piece of water that was surrounded by tall grass on all sides. It was the perfect place to hide. We settled in behind the grass and tried our duck call. After a few attempts we finally saw what we had been hoping for: a single duck flying in our direction. However, it happened so quickly that we barely had time to react.

We lifted our guns in unison and aimed at the duck.

The duck continued flying toward us.

We fired.

The next instant we were underwater. The kickback from the shotguns had knocked us backwards, and with the precarious balance of the canoe upset, we'd managed a less-than-graceful entry into the lagoon.

I had my gun in one hand, my paddle and the canoe in the other. Peter had dropped his gun, so he had to dive for it in the frigid water. After he retrieved it we swam in slow motion to a place where we could stand in the muck and water. We then proceeded to bail out our canoe.

It was a tough slog paddling back upstream. The combination of hard work and my wool pants probably prevented me from freezing, but when we finally reached the car our clothes were frozen solid. We started the car and cranked up the heat.

After our clothes had turned from solid ice to soggy rags, my companion turned to me and said, "You know, we don't have to tell anyone back at the dorm about what happened today."

And we didn't … until now.

Tim Billings is a Research Assistant and part time lobster fisherman in Maine. He still likes to hunt and paddle … just not at the same time.

The Loop

It will only hurt a little bit.

By Amy Attas

I named my steed Jazelle, for no reason but that it suited her. Five Alive pulled up lame, but was lame in the same bland, tolerable way at every breakdown, not unlike his jockey. Howie was dependable but a bit deficient in the personality department. Quiet Boy abstained from the name game, maybe because he was too cool for such foolishness, or maybe because he wasn't cool enough to think of one. And then there was C-Rash, who left a trail of misfortune and motorbike parts strewn across rural Laos.

We did The Loop. And we survived.

The first sign of trouble came shortly after C-Rash, Quiet Boy, and I arrived in Vientiane, the capitol of Laos, and reread the magazine clipping about The Loop that C-Rash had been carting around since Bangkok. It was just after eight in the evening, and we decided to find the motorbike rental shop first thing the next morning so we could hit the road by noon—we were on a schedule.

But then we consulted our guidebook and realized we were actually six hours from the town with the desired bike rental shop. Okay. Change the schedule.

The next day, on the ride to Tha Khaek, we met Five Alive and Howie and our bus got a flat tire. Another bad omen. But unlike a Canadian flat bus tire, which requires hours of waiting and probably a replacement bus, this one was fixed in twenty minutes by a handful of resourceful Lao passengers who changed the flat and got us rolling again. That was the real omen for The Loop: things will go wrong, but no single thing will be disastrous.

It was easy to find the motorbike rental shop and even easier to convince Mr. Ku that we knew how to drive them. We had no licenses—just cash, a smile, and a few pieces of ID. Then, on a test drive to the end of the dirt road, C-Rash hit a tree. This was how we learned that changing from third to second gear while attempting a U-turn can leave a bruise. Mr. Ku giggled apprehensively, handed us a hand-drawn map of the countryside with his emergency cell number scrawled on the back, then watched us jerk and sputter around the first bend in the road.

We stopped to check out a cave. From the roadside, a small boy led us through the brush to a stream that cut into a mountain. We tested the echo and I thought about Fraggles. Then we hopped back on our bikes to find a swimming hole. That's when Five Alive decided he wasn't going to respond to the electric or the kick-start.

After half an hour of fruitless searching for a mechanic, Five Alive's can-do Calgarian jockey had a try at his own solution. It worked: Five Alive was coaxed to life with a push and a stutter from second gear. For the next three days, we parked on top of a lot of hills.

While can-do Calgarian had been pleading with Five Alive, the rest of us had bolstered our motocross confidence exploring sandy side roads. When we hit the highway again, we ripped through the gear changes like race-car drivers, then pulled up full of swagger to make plans with a rejuvenated Five Alive.

But some of us forgot how to stop. That happened a lot—momentary mechanical amnesia. Coast onto the gravel, downshift, right foot on the brake (or was the left foot the brake?)—then, while cranking his throttle, Quiet Boy skids into the circle tumbling sideways.

"What happened?"

"Oh, I dunno."

"Are you okay?"

"Yeah."

"Is that blood?"

"Yeah. But this metal bit for my foot is bent now and I can't seem to change gears."

We smashed it with a rock to make room for the gearshift and got back on the road. Soon after, a butterfly flew into Howie's rider's helmet. Stop to avert insect massacre. Then Howie refused to turn over. Sigh. More rolling starts. Had Mr. Ku loaned us faulty equipment?

We coasted through the mountains, playing leapfrog as people stopped for photo opportunities, relishing the sun and the breeze and the I-can't-believe-I'm-here feeling.

Then we started to climb. Must have been a thirty-degree angle, and we leaned into the switchbacks feeling much more aggressive than our three hours of driving experience should have allowed.

C-Rash turned to me. "Should I be in third gear or second?"

"Uh, third."

Our bikes started to struggle.

"No wait, second."

"What?"

"Switch to second!"

C-Rash turned her gaze from me to her feet so she could press the heel of her flip-flop into the gearshift. She drifted onto the shoulder. She looked up. A basketball-sized boulder lay dead ahead. She panicked. I zipped past. When I looked back, she was in the ditch.

She looked healthy enough, standing next to her bike, so I took a picture before I turned back to help. Then a truck full of friendly locals pulled over to haul C-Rash back up to the pavement, and we pushed on.

Quiet Boy's engine seemed to be struggling with the altitude, but the rest of the group maintained momentum and telepathically agreed to rendezvous at the top to wait for him. We waited at the most visible gas station for half an hour. No Quiet Boy.

Five Alive went back down the hill, expecting to find him broken down or overheated on the shoulder. There was no trace. But we hadn't seen him at the top either. Was he lost in rural Laos? Our only hope was to continue to the guesthouse Mr. Ku had recommended for our first night and cross our fingers that Quiet Boy made it there, too. He'd figure that out, wouldn't he?

The road deteriorated from asphalt to packed gravel. It was under construction, and at times we bumbled through patches of loose sand where they'd been doing work. Howie stiffened her arms and stuck out her legs like training wheels. C-Rash tried holding her breath and cranking the throttle. I tried my best to look calm, but my wheels were unstable in the beach-like conditions, and slipping and tipping seemed imminent.

Then, without any warning whatsoever, we were in the middle of an active construction zone. I pulled left and drove over a ridge of sand to pass the grader, then held tight through the bumps. More machinery lay ahead, but I took a second to glance over my shoulder to check on the rest of the team. C-Rash, Five Alive, Howie, and … one extra pulling in behind. It was probably just a local, but the bike wasn't laden with cargo like most of the local bikes were. Dare I hope? Quiet Boy?

But there was no time to confirm my hopes—a massive truck was spraying water right in front of me, a steamroller was plowing just behind, and the grader had caught up. There was barely room to squeeze back to the right. The demands of Southeast Asia! You take a forty-kilometer drive off the main road and suddenly you're in a video game, swerving for your life. I bumbled through, then picked a regrouping spot as soon as I could to watch my team negotiate the machinery. No one got steamrolled.

"Quiet Boy! You're alive!"

"Yeah."

"What happened?"

"I took a wrong turn. But I called Mr. Ku and, well, now I'm here."

Couldn't argue with that.

We pushed on toward Tha Long, where the map showed a

place to sleep. We raced the setting sun, then stopped at a bridge to take a photo and check the map to see how much farther we had to go. Good thing: according to the map, the bridge was the first landmark after the town.

So we turned around, took a side road, and roamed the dirt tracks between bamboo huts looking for a guesthouse. No one spoke English, but everyone pointed us in the right direction— they knew where the gangs of Caucasian bikers wanted to go. Park the bikes, wash the dust off in the river, play a hand of cards, and collapse in a room barely big enough for the hard bed inside.

I got Quiet Boy to show me how to kickstart Jazelle in the morning, and she coughed to life on the third try. C-Rash didn't respond as kindly. But the guesthouse owner was friends with Mr. Ku and sent us across the road for aid. Half an hour and fifty thousand kip (about five dollars) later, C-Rash was ready for the road. And not a moment too soon, since we'd been warned that the road ahead was rough and we had a lot of distance to cover before the next guesthouse.

The road narrowed to barely the width of a car and the jungle appeared as a high green wall. We weaved through hills and around gaping potholes, standing on the foot pegs to properly enjoy the bumps. Some people had said this was the worst part of The Loop, but with a day's motorbike experience under our belts the dirt track was a fun new challenge. Click up to third gear, approach a corner, down to second, swerve left, right, dip into a hole, and burst out the other side. Pull right to heed a loaded five-ton truck. Stop at the first building in two hours to recollect the group.

There were other white people there, three jockeys whose steeds were called Red Racer, Evel Knievel, and Independent Francophone. Evel and Franco were fine, if a little peeved with the wait. Red Racer had just survived three hours of surgery to mend a broken chain. His jockey was nursing an allegedly broken rib after flying over the handlebars in an encounter with one of those "fun" potholes. He'd walked Red Racer for an hour to get to this mechanic. Now all was functioning, if not fit as a fiddle, and our group grew to eight.

I felt like Mother Goose for a while as I stayed back and corralled the stragglers, anticipating the next breakdown. But enough was enough, so I cranked the throttle and took the lead. Caution to wind … until I came up on a lumbering dump truck spitting up dust.

I pulled out to see about passing. I couldn't see a thing. I pulled back in. A car rattled past. I pulled out again. Still no visibility. C'mon, Mother Goose. Finally, I mustered the courage, revved up, and started climbing through the gears as I blasted past. The dust cleared. Shit. Straight in front of me the road disappeared into a truck-sized pothole. Drive in? Swerve around? Pull back?

I did all three.

My right hand worked overtime, twisting the throttle and squeezing the front brake. Poor Jazelle. She hit the dirt and I tumbled after. I broke the skid with my hands before realizing they were getting scratched to bits, so I lifted them and pulled into a roll in the middle of the road.

"Nice one." Red Racer was the first on the scene. "That roll was sweet."

I wrapped my bandana around my bleeding palm and readjusted my helmet in Jazelle's now-cracked side mirror. I tried the electric start. Dead silence. Kick-start? Success. Onward ho.

According to Mr. Ku's map, there was a cold spring just off The Loop. We followed the signs for Ban Na Phua, then followed our intuition to a rickety bridge with loose planks. We put our hands on our hips and assessed the situation. The bridge was low, so the fall wouldn't be fatal, but was it worth drowning a bike?

We were only forty percent sure this was the right way. Then some Lao girls arrived and squealed their motorbikes across, proving that it was possible. But was it worth it?

Evel Knievel gave it a shot. He made it.

I walked Jazelle down the hill to the bridge. Her front tire got stuck in a rut, so I kicked her started and twisted the throttle. She leapt forward. I grabbed that wicked hand brake and we tipped over into the dirt. Harmless, right? Wrong. My shin oozed blood, Jazelle's throttle no longer switched to OFF, and when I finally kicked her started on the eleventh try, black smoke started billowing skyward.

Then there was Quiet Boy. He ended up knee-deep in water, looking up at his bike as it lay flat on the bridge.

Howie didn't even attempt the crossing.

The cold spring was a gorgeous blue pool nestled in limestone. Worth every drop of spilled blood. And there was a lot of blood. After my fall, Howie's driver sliced her foot on the cliff as she was diving off; then Quiet Boy bruised his foot while trying to kick-start C-Rash, whose engine had flooded again. I spent five minutes leaning into the kickstarter before it finally budged; five sweet-talking minutes later, C-Rash coughed back to life. Nevertheless, we beamed as we rolled back to the main road in the late-afternoon glow, waving and shouting "*Sabaidee!*" to the naked kids who ran across the road.

At night the group bonded over sticky rice and spicy papaya salad, a meal Evel Knievel claimed was a local delicacy. And the next morning we woke with the sun to check out the three-hour boat ride through Konglor Cave. C-Rash didn't start. My sweet-talking had lost its power. We dropped him off at yet another mechanic and C-Rash's jockey rode with me to the caves.

For most, the highlight of a visit to Konglor Cave would be either the ride in a vintage leaky boat, the moments of echoing voices in pure darkness, or the walk through glowing orange stalactites and stalagmites. Those things were all stunning, but for our crew, Red Racer's collision with a tree in front of a huge local audience might have overshadowed it all. With a bent front basket and a bruised ego, Red Racer underscored why Mr. Ku's bikes were in such rough shape.

The road out of Ban Konglor was flat and straight, and with the highway ahead oft described as smooth and boring, we held out hope that all disasters were behind us. For the last time, we squished eight plastic chairs around a low table for lunch in a one-room, one-dish restaurant. Afterward, fully fed, we splintered off with plans to meet at a guesthouse in Tha Khaek.

But C-Rash wasn't finished. Three days of mechanical mishaps and repairs meant his bolts were loose, and just after our last fuel stop his side panel snapped off. A bit of a shock, but nothing his jockey couldn't hold together until we found another mechanic.

The last hour back to Tha Khaek was easy … actually, no. Red Racer's chain snapped again. At least this time his jockey could repair it himself.

Then C-Rash pulled over. The bike wouldn't go. Flooded engine? Oil leak? Loose screws? Ah, no, just budget travel and back luck. Out of gas.

A preteen at the house down the road dumped a Fanta bottle of fuel into the tank and, save for a few swerves around dogs, pigs, and chickens, we were home free. Hell's Angels shone down on us long enough to navigate Tha Khaek back to Mr. Ku's shop, where we shared beers and horror stories with the ignorant fools about to set out on The Loop.

The moral of our story? Do the Loop.

Amy Attas has been paid to shovel dirt, pick cherries, play with children, and make movies. She writes, too, and sometimes she gets paid for that. She's presently polishing a novel about tree planting while nursing motorcycle wounds on her parents' couch in Pinawa, Manitoba.

Jambon

Somewhere, an accordion began to play.

By Steve Pitt

I once did a cooks' tour of France with some fellow trainee chefs. Being the only non-teenager in the group, after a few days I felt the need for at least one meal without being asked to "Pass the salt, dude." I finally got my chance in the town of Beaune where, owing to a one-day French bus strike, we unexpectedly found ourselves with half a day to wander around on our own.

I immediately snuck off for a solitary lunch. In a matter of minutes, I found a picture-perfect French restaurant, complete with waiters in handlebar mustachios and starched white aprons the size of China clipper mainsails.

The regional specialty of Beaune is escargot. Well, who can resist a chance to eat snails? A half-liter of wine and a basket of crispy still-oven-warm bread arrived first. One bite, one sip, and I was ready to put down roots for life.

After a few minutes, a striking, well-dressed woman in her late thirties entered the restaurant twirling a cigarette holder in one hand and a leash on the other. At the end of the cigarette holder was a lit cigarette. At the end of the leash was an ancient boxer (the canine variety, not the pugilist sort). She called her dog something like "Jambon," and it waddled painfully behind her like a dutiful sugar daddy. In France, cigarettes and dogs are still allowed in restaurants. The dogs generally smell better.

Madame took a seat at the nearest table with her back immediately to me. Jambon dutifully settled down under her chair. Already waiting for her was a young man in his twenties wearing a badly wrinkled Harris Tweed coat and shiny black pants. He was sporting the worst comb-over I have ever seen.

Being France, it could have been l'amour, but more likely it was just an elegant woman lunching with her dorky stamp-licking bureaucrat nephew. Whatever the reason, the one thing they definitely had in common was smoking. As they chatted incessantly, huge clouds of smoke rolled my way. Just so you know, French cigarettes smell like burning mummies.

Being Canadian, I endured it in silence. Besides, I was geared up for my escargot.

For those who have ever dined on escargot in North America, please note that the rubbery, pathetic little overpriced slugs they serve there bear no resemblance to the homegrown variety of Burgundy, France. In most North American restaurants, snots (trade name for snails) come in cans. The contents are heated in a microwave, stuffed into pre-owned snail shells, then given a deep-sea burial in a greasy sauce, usually from the same can.

In France, escargots are picked fresh from the field, detoxified for forty-eight hours, cooked in their shells, then covered in a super-rich garlic-butter sauce. Because these snails are still anchored to their homes, the French have invented special tools to evict them. You get a spring-and-claw thingy that grabs the shell like a surgeon's clamp, along with an elegant two-pronged pick that you stab into the meat and pull.

The waiter slid a dimpled dish bearing six escargots in front of me with a flourish, bowing and snapping a napkin. Being a complete novice at snail-picking, it took me at least a minute to grasp the shell in my clamp, jab in the pick, and slowly but firmly pry my first juicy escargot out of its shell.

I raised my impaled snot to find that I was not dining alone. Smelling food, Jambon had abandoned his station at the foot of Madame's chair, jumped up on the chair opposite me, and commenced ogling me and my lunch with a love-struck stare that you could find only in France.

I cleared my throat a couple of times, trying to get the attention of Jambon's owner. When at last she noticed my phlegmy hints, she did nothing more than contemptuously light another flaming Tut.

Ignoring Jambon's unblinking gaze, I chowed down on my first snail. Indescribable, the way that garlic butter hits you. I stabbed into my second one. Jambon, perhaps thinking that somehow I hadn't noticed him, emitted a low whimper of sweet longing that would have done Maurice Chevalier proud. No dice, Monsieur Bow-Wow. The second escargot met the same fate as the first.

Escargot number three put up a fight. Or maybe my hands were just a tad shaky because Jambon was now talking to me. Or at least he was opening and closing his mouth and making "maa-maa-maa" sounds, punctuated by longing moans. So call the French SPCA; I ate the third snot, too.

At escargot number four, Jambon must have decided that I just couldn't see him through the clouds of purple smoke. So he slammed his huge head on the table with a loud thunk, jowls fanning out on each side like pancakes. Snail fork poised in the air, I made the mistake of looking him in the eyes. Huge, brown, unbelievably sad eyes. Somewhere, an accordion began to play. A tear seemed to form at the side of one of Jambon's eyes and his lips stretched in a long black line nearly eight inches across, quivering as if they were about to break out in heart-rending sobs.

I couldn't stand it! I served him a quick snot on a piece of French bread. He gobbled it down in one bite and then looked hopefully at the remaining two snails.

Damn, I thought. I just realized that I had set a precedent. Fortunately, the first three escargots had been incredibly filling, so I decided we could split the difference. I gulped down the fifth snail, then picked up a six-inch stick of French bread, smeared it end to end with the last of the garlic butter, and topped it with the final snail. Without dropping so much as a crumb, Jambon took the baguette out of my hand and tilted his head back. In one motion, the bread slid out of sight with the band still playing "Nearer My God to Thee."

The food gone, Jambon abandoned his chair and returned to his place under his mistress. Not so much as a thank-you. Not even a backward glance. Harrumph. The French. I finished my wine, had dessert and coffee, received and paid the bill, and got up to leave.

Just then, both Madame and companion simultaneously stopped chatting. They wrinkled their noses in horror and scanned the restaurant for the offender.

They glanced at me, but I was too far away. They glared at their nearest neighbors, who protested their innocence. Finally, they looked under the table at Jambon, who was asleep. His tail and toes twitched as if he was having a dog dream. It wasn't a dog dream.

Madame and her table companion wrinkled their noses once again, the waiter flapped his apron, and everyone else dabbed their eyes with their napkins and complained to Madame about her dog. I assumed my best Gallic snoot and headed for the door.

Time for a little fresh air, dude.

Steve Pitt has been a professional writer for more than 30 years. In 1980 he won a Periodical Distributors Author's Award for humor for an article that appeared in Harrowsmith *magazine. In addition to being a writer, Steve Pitt has worked as a movie extra, army reserve soldier, dishwasher, farm hand, martial arts instructor, bartender, youth outreach worker, armored truck guard, Yukon gold prospector, manager of a shelter for homeless men, goose rancher, lay minister, bar bouncer, resort cook and stay-at-home dad. You'll find him in cyberspace at www.stevepitt.ca.*

Swimmer Support

Things that go bump on the lake.

By Bill Miller

Every Labor Day weekend, there is a swimming race across Lake Waccamaw in North Carolina. My fourteen-year-old son Daniel was on his high school swim team and decided he was up for the challenge.

The distance is a little over eight kilometers, and sometimes the water can be quite rough with plenty of whitecaps when you get near the middle of the lake. Such was the case on this particular year. The sky was overcast, temperatures were cool, and there were fifteen-to-twenty-knot winds blowing out of the northwest.

For reasons of safety, each swimmer is required to have a support boat. Never having been to the event, I had figured the seventeen-foot Coleman canoe I had borrowed from a friend would more than suffice.

Everyone else, it turned out, had motorized boats.

Race participants were young and old, male and female. Because the air temperature was only fifteen degrees Celsius (sixty degrees Fahrenheit) everyone was anxious to get moving. After the pistol fired it didn't take long for the field to spread out, and as the race progressed I was proud to see that Daniel was holding his own.

To help guide boats and participants, the race organizers had placed five-foot-high marker buoys about every one-and-a-half kilometers along the route. As I found out the following year—when I was the swimmer—you can't see the shoreline from the water for most of the race because the surrounding topography is so flat. For that reason swimmers rely on the marker buoys and the direction of their support boats to guide them on the shortest route across the lake.

The canoe turned out to be a problem. Because the wind was blowing hard, I was forced to constantly correct the angle of the bow from twenty degrees east to twenty degrees west. Needless to say, Daniel soon noticed how our direction seemed to be changing constantly in relation to the other support boats. He decided it might be best if I followed him for a while, and that he would guide himself using either the markers (if he could see one) or another boat that was keeping a straighter line. I thought this was a good idea, so I pulled in behind and started to follow him.

Since this is a relatively long race, I became distracted after a while, and started daydreaming and looking at the other boats and swimmers.

Then I hit something. I heard a loud *thud!* followed by a series of equally loud thumping noises as I continued paddling over top of the obstacle. I could not imagine what I had run over in twenty feet of water—although on nice days you sometimes see alligators on the surface basking in the sun.

It turned out the obstacle was my not-so-happy son.

Because Daniel was able to swim in a much straighter line than I could paddle, we decided it was still best for me to follow him. About a half-hour later I heard the same sickening *thud!* This time I knew what it was, but it was too late to do anything about it. In an effort to get over him as quickly as possible, I dug deep with my paddle and managed to catch his arm with the paddle blade.

Daniel, ever the diplomat, said he thought it might improve our chances of winning the race if I would "Go and help someone else." Since this was against the rules, I was not able to take him up on his suggestion, and despite my unintentional efforts to immobilize my son in the middle of the lake, he did end up crossing the finish line.

As mentioned, I participated in the same swimming race the following year, and I asked a friend to go along with Daniel in the support canoe to help him stay focused. I didn't want him running over anything or anyone unintentionally.

I finished the swim without being hit once. I guess the moral of the story is that you can sometimes trust friends more than family.

Bill Miller is an avid kayaker who is grateful that he wasn't "steamrolled" by a canoe during his own swim across Lake Waccamaw.

Red Devil

An encounter with the most unsavory creature in the northern woods.

By David Lee

There exists an unpredictable Dr.-Jekyll-and-Mr.-Hyde-type creature that inhabits most of North America's vast forestland. During most encounters it will be skittish—but if you unwittingly cross paths with this forest dweller at the wrong time, you may come face-to-face with a brazen and petulant beast.

It is small, but don't let that fool you—it has large, powerful claws, and it can use them to tear the ground apart or scale trees in an effortless bound. It has equally large and powerful incisors, strong enough to shred or cut through the hardiest of materials. Its agility is second to none. It can move at lightning speed and leap incredible distances. Its acrobatics and aerial maneuvers are in the domain of superheroes.

What is this devilish creature, you may ask? The seemingly innocuous red squirrel!

It was a perfect August day when I set out with my former girlfriend Marylou on a multi-day backpacking trip in Algonquin Provincial Park, Ontario's oldest and best-loved wilderness park. We were walking the Western Uplands trail and had chosen a figure-eight loop that we could cover comfortably in eight days.

For the first few days, we were lucky. We spotted a black bear from a close but safe distance, heard wolves howling nearby, and even had a moose wander through our campsite one morning. It's rare that you can experience close (and safe) encounters with the many wildlife species that call this wilderness home, so we certainly weren't expecting more in the way of wildlife sightings.

On our third evening, we arrived at the small lake where we would camp. It wasn't a lake to get particularly excited about, at least compared to the one we had camped at the previous night. That one had come with a perfect rocky point, clear water for swimming, and even a sandy beach. This one was small and narrow and had plenty of weeds choking its dark, murky waters. Four campsites were strung along the southern shore of the lake; hoping to maintain some semblance of privacy, we opted for the last site.

We followed our usual routine for the rest of the day, pitching our tent, washing ourselves, feeding our calorie-starved bodies, and then sitting down to relax. However, we never completely relaxed until we had completed one of the most important duties of the day: hanging the food bag in a tree to prevent bears from stumbling into our campsite and making off with our edibles.

Many campsites lacked big trees or firm branches, but today our setup was bombproof. We hoisted the food bag high in a tree, far from any branches, and then stood back and admired our work. The bag swung like a pendulum—a real thing of beauty.

The heat and humidity made sleep difficult that night, but eventually we dozed off. The next morning we slept in, wakened only by a most terrible sound in the trees above. My partner froze as I put a finger to my lips.

I craned my neck to listen more intently and heard it again … the unmistakable sound of teeth ripping fabric.

"That's our food bag!" I shouted. Within seconds, clothes and camping paraphernalia were flying in every direction. I scrambled out of the tent, hopped around for a few seconds with one sandal on, and then spotted the red devil himself, his teeth deep into the waterproof fabric of our food bag.

"Hey!" I yelled. "That's our food bag!" The squirrel glared at me and peppered the morning air with shrill chatter.

As I wondered what to do, it occurred to me that I was standing outside without any clothes on. I looked around for prying eyes; finding none, I turned my attention back to the matter at hand.

I searched the campsite for something to throw; finding nothing, I pulled off my sandals. The first toss missed completely, but the second sandal came close enough to momentarily dissuade the squirrel. Encouraged, I began shouting threats, doing my best to look and sound like a naked barbarian. The squirrel decided to make his escape. He shimmied partway up the rope and made an incredible leap to freedom. James Bond would have been proud.

After dressing, I lowered the food bag and found an inch-long tear in the fabric. I was glad the squirrel hadn't reached the food—I couldn't imagine the carnage it would have caused had it reached the trail mix.

After having breakfast and packing up camp, we made our way back to the trail. We passed a father and son at their campsite and gave our usual backpackers' salutation. The father responded politely, but the fact that his response that included the words "after I patch this damn pack" stopped us in our tracks.

Over the next few minutes, he regaled us about the red squirrel that had torn a sizeable hole in their food bag and eaten most of their peanuts. Earlier that morning, he had heard strange noises coming from the hanging food bag. He had quickly lowered it, and as the pack hit the ground, a squirrel's head popped out of the hole with its cheeks full of nuts. Before the father could do anything, the squirrel leaped from the bag and dashed into the woods with his cheeks full of loot.

It was hard to believe that a single squirrel could terrorize two campsites, but really, was there another logical conclusion? We wished the father and son well and continued on our way.

As we walked past the last campsite, we glanced down toward the water and stopped in our tracks. Below was a visibly distressed couple sifting through even greater carnage. My partner and I looked at each other and went down for a look. It's like that deer-in-the-headlights phenomenon—you want to look away, but you just can't bring yourself to do so.

The couple confirmed our suspicion: they had been visited by a dastardly red squirrel that had turned their campsite into a crime scene. As with the father and son, the beast had chewed its way into their waterproof food bag, tearing off chunks of the material like it was ripping paper. The forest floor below the food bag was covered with pieces of purple vinyl and nuts, and the hole in the bag was big enough for an army of squirrels to pass through!

This squirrel obviously had a chip on his shoulder; the rascal didn't need a hole that big, but he was determined to send a message.

When they were wakened, the young couple had followed the same course of action the rest of us had, yelling at the chattering animal and throwing footwear at it. When the squirrel carried on undeterred, they lowered the tattered food bag to chase it off. That was when the squirrel leapt from the descending pack, deftly navigated through the debris on the forest floor, landed in the fire pit, and then propelled itself onto another bench where the couple had placed their Platypus hydration pack.

In an act of true defiance, the squirrel stood erect, chattered contemptuously, and then bit hard into the bulging Platypus before running off into the woods. In its wake, it left a Platypus spewing water like a fire hydrant.

As outdoors people, we're accustomed to hearing stories about close encounters with bears and moose. Little did I know their woodland cousin, *Tamiasciurus hudsonicus*—the red squirrel—might sport the worst attitude of them all.

Despite being shaken by this incident, David continues to venture forth into the red squirrel's domain, wondering if it will ever strike again. He is a passionate paddler, photographer, speaker and writer who likes sharing stories from his many adventures at ***passionatepaddler.blogspot.com***.

The Name Game

Naming other people's children is an art form.

By Darin Cook

My wife and I were newlyweds when we left for South Korea to teach English, and we promised our families we wouldn't procreate any children of our own while living abroad. This was an easy promise to make, as one of the reasons we were traveling was to delay domesticity. And after the first few days of our new careers—experiencing firsthand the energy and patience needed to control dozens of rowdy kids—having children of our own was the furthest thing from our minds.

That didn't stop us from thinking about baby names, however. We were surprised to learn that naming children in South Korea is not only a parental duty, but that foreign teachers in ESL schools are responsible for giving English names to students who don't already have one.

Indeed, on my very first day in the classroom there was a new student who didn't have an English name, so my Korean teaching partner instructed me to give him one. Just like that: No planning, no consulting a baby name book, no negotiating with the child's parents. So I named him Willy, for no other reason than I was under pressure to come up with something on the spot.

It's one thing to name your own baby. But as new students continued to enroll in our classes, it became an almost daily requirement to come up with names.

I worried about giving out unpopular or laughable names. One trick I used was to ask the student his or her Korean name and then make an English name that sounded similar. Thus, Sujin became Susan. Or sometimes a Korean name had a meaning from which we could formulate an English name. For instance, my wife's first new student had a Korean name that meant "pearl," so thereafter she became known as Pearl.

Of course, this didn't always work, and as this naming spree continued throughout the school term, we often had to get creative to come up with English identities for scores of young Korean students. It wasn't surprising that our school began sounding like our hometown back in Canada: there was Liam, Evelyn, Andy, and Jack. It turned out that we didn't need a baby name book after all; we just dredged up familiar names to make our school feel more like home.

Real Korean names are chosen for auspicious reasons to honor both the individual and the family. Each name is composed of three parts, beginning with the family name, followed by a generational name, and then an individual name. What my wife and I were doing by naming students Ace and Frankie didn't seem to fit with Korean tradition. Nevertheless, it was a requirement of being educated in an English school—and it didn't take long for the students to figure out that they could pick their own English names. Several boys had already picked out the name Harry for themselves. The Harry Potter novels and movies have all been translated into Korean, and naturally, they all wanted to replicate the moniker of their favorite pint-sized wizard.

After the first three months, some of the students who had been at the school for a while began changing their names. They weren't dissatisfied with the names we'd given them, but were simply becoming more comfortable in an English-speaking environment and setting out to reinvent themselves. They had discovered that English names were a transient identity for classroom purposes, and that if a teacher could change a Korean name to an English name, they could just as easily change from one English name to another.

One of my most memorable students decided he would like to be called HappyMeal. This seemed to start a whole new movement. Two others soon decided to change their names to CocaCola and ChocolateMilk.

Also appearing were English-sounding words that could be construed as names, but were more likely just snappier to say, such as Kez, Kephi, and Kixx. These kids could rename themselves as though they were giving themselves wacky aliases for Facebook or MySpace. Even if their English names tended toward the goofy side, they had their original Korean names to fall back on when not in English class.

This name-changing craze hit its peak when I realized that one of my young female students might be having an identity crisis. When I had first arrived at the school, her name was June. After a month she changed it to Youme, which lasted two weeks until she went back to June. A few days later, Sady became her name of choice, which I feared could change at any moment.

She seemed bothered when asked what her name was on any given day; maybe it was a translation problem in her own mind, as if she wasn't satisfied with any of the English words that were supposed to describe her. I told her June was a perfect name for her and she went back to that, maybe taking comfort that an English speaker approved of it.

This was all consistent with the respect shown for ESL teachers, because in Korea there is a strong emphasis on learning English. Receiving a new, possibly temporary, name is part of that education. When parents hear that little Park Kyeong Hee is also known as Jennifer, they feel content that their child is one step closer to being educated in the English language.

Darin Cook is a freelance writer based in London, Ontario. He draws material for his travel essays and other works of non-fiction from his life's varied experiences. His travels have provided him the opportunity to successfully teach English in South Korea, as well as to study the Korean language himself, with much less success. Darin has never changed his name, although he likes the thought of being called Indiana.

Up the Creek

Without a paddle … or a boat … or a video camera. You get the picture.

By Ben Coxworth

We were four unsuspecting souls paddling Alberta's Upper Red Deer River that day. Fellow paddler Kevin and I were in our whitewater kayaks, and our friends Rick and Cindy were in Cindy's brand-new canoe. Just for fun, I'd brought along my new handheld video camera, which I had carefully sealed in a jerry-rigged, chest-mounted waterproof housing.

The Upper Red Deer is a beautiful stretch of river, with sections of rapids that usually run at about Class II or Class III. It's fun, but not usually scary. However, when Rick and Cindy had run it a few weeks earlier, the water had been unexpectedly high and they had capsized and lost Rick's canoe. They figured they would come back again when the water had dropped to normal levels. That day was today.

When we arrived at the put-in, we could see that the river was still running fairly high. Our confidence was not boosted when the first rumbles of thunder sounded to the west; once we pushed onto the water, we could see a big storm rolling in our direction. I've been caught paddling in thunderstorms before, and it's not enjoyable. You either risk electrocution by staying on the water, or you run into the woods in your soaking-wet neoprene and proceed to sit there with your teeth chattering until the storm passes.

This time, however, the storm was content to boom at us a little before moving on. We figured that was a good omen for the day ahead.

The Upper Red Deer has a fun whitewater feature called *Gooseberries*. That is to say, it's *usually* fun. It's a river-wide ledge that's two or three feet high, which can most often be navigated just about anywhere. Still, sensible paddlers always get out and scout it first, to make sure nothing has changed.

As we studied the ledge from shore, we could see that the high water level had turned the usually good-natured spillover into a nasty recirculating hydraulic—a water feature that can grab a kayak, pull the boat and its occupant under the surface, and then spin them around for a while before (hopefully) spitting them out again.

Experienced paddlers call such an experience "getting Maytagged," as the paddler gets spun around as if they're in a washing machine. Unfortunately, it's often hard to tell how long a hydraulic might hold a paddler under the surface. Some of them—these ones are called "keepers"—never spit out what they pull in. Given that, we decided that the only safe place to run the ledge would be at a sedate little chute on the far left-hand side of the river.

Kevin and I went first. I paddled several feet behind him with my video camera in hand, watching nervously as he paddled toward the chute. As he disappeared over the ledge, I did pretty much the worst thing possible in such a situation: I capsized.

I don't know how it happened, other than that the swirling water immediately before the ledge must have upset my delicate equilibrium. I was now being swept upside down toward a feature that we were all afraid of running right side up.

I frantically raised my paddle up along the side of my kayak and executed a sloppy, desperate Eskimo roll. I got back up before reaching the ledge, but here's the thing about doing a roll in turbulent water: when you get topside, you're often disoriented, and it usually takes a second or two to figure out which way you're facing. In this case, that second or two was all it took for me to reach the point of no return. By the time I figured out where I was going, it was too late to reach the chute.

It's an awful feeling, seeing a rocky ledge coming toward you and not knowing what's on the other side. All you know is that it's going to be nasty. As I crested the ledge, I got a brief glimpse of a lot of foamy whitewater below the drop, which the boat and I nosed hard into.

No sooner had my kayak cleared the ledge and stalled in the foam than the powerful force of the river slammed onto the stern like a giant fist. The boat and I were yanked violently backward, and then pummeled down into the hydraulic.

In the chaos that ensued, it was almost impossible to tell if I was upside down or sideways, but I attempted a roll nonetheless. It didn't even come close to working. Ordinarily I would try again, but in this case I just wanted to be out of there as fast as possible, so I decided to swim for it. Reaching toward my waist, I madly groped for the release cord of my spray skirt, the neoprene thingy that keeps water out of the cockpit of the kayak (and also keeps you in it). I yanked it off using the accompanying strap, then sort of somersaulted forward and thrashed my way out of the boat.

As my head broke the surface, I realized that *Gooseberries* was roaring away only a few feet behind me. Not wanting to get pulled back in, I grabbed my boat and started swimming downstream and toward the riverbank. Usually it's pretty easy to swim your boat ashore in the slower, deeper stretch of river immediately after *Gooseberries*. Today, however, I wasn't going to make it. I stayed with my kayak until I saw another rocky ledge approaching, at which point I cut my losses, let go of my boat and began swimming for the shore in earnest.

I soon reached the riverbank; as I looked downstream I could see that Kevin had paddled out to my mostly submerged kayak and was struggling to push it ashore using the nose of his boat. He gave a valiant effort, but eventually had to give up. As I watched my boat disappear around a distant bend in the river, I wondered if I would ever see it again—and whether I'd really mind that much if I didn't.

Rick and Cindy soon arrived in their canoe and stopped to pick me up. The only place for me to sit was on the "floor" of their boat, not unlike a small child would. We proceeded down the river, and before long we reached another set of rapids known as *Jimbo's Staircase*.

I don't know who Jimbo is, or was, but it's called a staircase because it consists of a series of ledges that eager paddlers can drop over, one after the other. Again, like *Gooseberries*, it's usually fun. Emphasis on the word *usually*.

As we paddled into the rapids, it immediately became obvious that my extra weight was causing the canoe to ride too low: water began slopping over the gunwales and into the boat. One of the larger ledges was coming up, and I realized our canoe was not going to be light enough to bounce over it. This was apparently on Rick's mind as well. He let loose with, "Crap, we're not gonna make it!"—an accurate appraisal of our situation.

The boat skidded halfway over the ledge, and then abruptly stopped. A moment later, unable to withstand the water pressure, the canoe *folded* in half.

Cindy was now below the ledge, still sitting in the bow. Rick was above the ledge, still sitting in the stern. But I was sitting *on* the ledge.

To make matters much worse, I was trapped there. The thwart, a structural-support board that runs width-wise across the middle of the canoe, was being pressed down by the folding action of the boat, thereby trapping my legs underneath it.

While the rushing water poured over and around the back of the canoe, Rick leapt out and planted his feet on the rocks above the ledge, trying with Herculean effort to pull the boat sideways. It took a few hard tugs, but he eventually moved the canoe off the protrusion it was stuck on, which allowed me just enough room to pull myself free.

"Get out!" he shouted.

I didn't need to be told twice. I jumped ship and swam hard for shore, with Cindy hot on my heels.

Now that its load was lightened, the canoe swept clear of the ledge. As it did so, it miraculously popped back into shape. Cindy knew that we needed the swamped boat, so she swam over and grabbed onto it as the canoe floated downstream. Kevin chased after the two of them in his kayak.

Once Rick and I had swum to shore (déjà vu!), we started walking down the slippery, ankle-twisting shoreline to catch up with Cindy. We were glad to see that she had managed to get ashore safely, but there was one problem with where she did it: It was on the far side of the river from where Rick and I were stranded.

We knew that wading across would be impossible, and swimming or drifting with the current would be foolhardy. We gave some thought to hanging onto the back of Kevin's kayak and having him ferry me across, but given the chaotic conditions, this idea sounded like another disaster waiting to happen.

As we contemplated our next move, I suddenly realized that my video camera was missing. I hadn't even thought about it for who knows how long. It was probably on its way to Hudson's Bay by now, but just so I could say that I checked, I decided to walk back along the section of river we'd just paddled. To my surprise, I found it floating in a pool of water, scenes of insanity presumably embedded on its memory card.

By the time I'd stuffed the camera into my dry top, a solution to our transportation problem had pulled up directly across the river: several boatloads of novice whitewater rafters were stopping for a break. I tried yelling at them, but couldn't make myself heard over the thunderous churning of the rapids. Communicating with my waving arms, however, I managed to get the attention of one of their guides, who motioned that they would pick me up when they were ready to leave. Rick joined me again, and after a few minutes the rafters picked us up.

So, did anything crazy happen with the rafts? Did one of them get pierced by a sharp rock and deflate while flying around like a big balloon? No, this story isn't quite *that* good. (Although I do think some of the rafters were quite excited to be part of a rescue mission.)

In any case, we soon reached our prearranged take-out at a place called the S-Bend. And wouldn't you know it: sitting on a gravel bar right in front of the take-out beach was my kayak. Someone must have seen it floating past, waded in, and pulled it up on shore.

When I got home, I loaded the video footage from *Gooseberries* onto my computer. It didn't look like much. As soon as I slipped over the ledge, the camera had recorded a lot of dark, green water and white foam. There were no fish staring at me with puzzled expressions, no sunken treasure chests.

I decided I didn't want any mementos of the event, so I deleted it.

The next day at work, I told one of my co-workers the story. He listened intently to every word, and when I had finished, he exclaimed, "Wow, I wish something like that would happen to *me*!"

I think it must have gained something in the telling.

Ben Coxworth is fresh out of a career in television production, and now works as a writer and editor for Gizmag Emerging Technology Magazine. *He still has his whitewater kayak, although he hasn't used it much lately. He lives in Edmonton, Alberta, and can be contacted at* **coxworth@shaw.ca**.

Airport Charade

What happens when you trust the smiling lady in a wheelchair?

By Margrit de Graff

"My daughter Valerie and I had been dreaming for a long time of riding our bicycles through Europe. So we bought plane tickets, read books about cycling routes through Germany, Austria, Switzerland, and France, and exercised for many months to prepare ourselves. Finally the day arrived when we would leave.

The plan was this: Valerie would board a plane in Vancouver and I would join her on the same aircraft when it landed in Edmonton to pick up more passengers on the way to Frankfurt, Germany. Another of my daughters, Kathy, works at the airport in Edmonton. Kathy, who hadn't seen her sister in a while, wanted to take this opportunity to visit for a few moments.

"You can't do that," I said. "You know that passengers in transit can't get off the airplane."

"Don't worry about it," Kathy replied. "I have a plan."

I've raised my children to be independent thinkers, and as we drove to the airport I wondered what plan she'd worked out. At the airport she stopped between several taxis lined up on the departure level (a big no-no), jumped out, and ran for the front door, shouting over her shoulder, "Stay in the car! I'll be right back!"

Moments later I saw her coming through the revolving doors … pushing a wheelchair!

"You must be kidding!"

"It's okay, Mom," she said. "Just sit in this chair while I park the car."

She hastily piled all my bicycle gear on my lap—four panniers, a small backpack, and my bicycle helmet on top like a cherry—and drove off toward the car park. As people walked by, they smiled at the poor invalid in her wheelchair, accompanied by all the cycling paraphernalia. People were very nice, and the odd juxtaposition of wheelchair and bicycle gear didn't seem to faze anyone.

Kathy reappeared a few minutes later, grabbed the wheelchair, and began pushing me to the check-in counter. The attendant greeted us, and as she began checking me in she turned to Kathy and asked, "Can she walk?"

"No, she can't," said Kathy.

I couldn't believe that the attendant didn't address me directly. The nerve!

The plus side, of course, was that I was sitting in comfort and didn't have to lug my baggage around. Getting pushed to the right places by someone who knew the airport inside and out definitely had a certain appeal.

We lined up to get through security. Kathy knew the uniformed women behind the counter, and she introduced me as her mom who was flying to Frankfurt. They looked at me with only slight interest, and one of them asked my daughter if I was flying alone. Kathy confirmed that I was.

I wheeled myself closer to the counter and placed my little backpack and bike helmet on top. The women looked at me, then at my baggage, and the penny dropped. One of the women said in disbelief, "*She's* going backpacking?"

Kathy had to think quickly. "No, she's going cycling," she said. "She broke her leg and can't walk very well yet ... but she can ride a bike."

The security staff exchanged glances, but let me pass. Kathy pushed me to the metal detector, and the young man operating it bent down and asked in a friendly tone, "Can you stand?"

Happy to be addressed directly, I replied, "I can sure try." I leaned heavily on the armrests of the wheelchair and heaved myself out. Slowly, carefully, I straightened myself out until I stood upright, mostly on my left leg. (I reminded myself not to forget which leg was the bad one!)

In an apologetic voice, the young man asked, "Can you turn around like this?" To be honest, I was rather enjoying the charade by now. I must have put on a good show, for he thanked me politely and let us pass.

We made it through the gate just fine, and as Kathy pushed me toward the airplane we heard a stewardess laughing. She was talking with another woman, and they both turned when they saw a wheelchair approaching. The other woman was my daughter Valerie.

The laughter died on my daughter's lips. As we approached, Valerie said lamely to the stewardess, "That's my mom!"

"Oh!" the stewardess said, surprised. Then: "*She's* going to cycle all over Europe?"

I answered quickly, "I broke my leg a while back and can't walk very well yet, but cycling is all right."

Valerie's expression was a mixture of worry and puzzlement. She and Kathy lifted me out of the wheelchair, and I leaned heavily on the backs of every seat as they carried me along the aisle of the plane to my seat. I didn't explain the situation until we were airborne.

Several hours later, as we disembarked from the plane in Frankfurt, we noticed a fellow in airport uniform waiting at the gates with a wheelchair. I walked past him, feeling guilty—they would probably search the entire plane for the handicapped lady who had magically disappeared during the flight.

Valerie and I spent five great weeks cycling through Europe. Some areas were extremely demanding, and we pedaled and pushed our heavily loaded bikes up many a steep mountain road. We fell into a deep, exhausted sleep every night, but got in better shape with every day. We felt exuberant and on top of the world when our trip was finished and we had to return to Frankfurt to fly home.

At the airport, we walked up to the young attendant and joked with him as he helped us pack our bikes for the flight home. When it was time to check in, I put my bike bags on the conveyor, and the attendant looked up my name on his computer. A strange look crossed his face.

He looked at me, looked at my passport, then leaned closer to the screen. Finally he turned to me and said with incredulity, *"You need a wheelchair?"*

At Margrit's age she knows that she can get away with anything—and she takes full advantage of it! She recently returned from a round-the-world voyage on a freighter, where she turned to writing after her first feeble attempts at conversing with the all-Russian crew. You can read about her on the history page of De Graff's Eco Resort (www.degraffs.com), or e-mail her at margritdegraff@yahoo.ca.

Cape Tormentine

Surviving one's youth at a cottage on Northumberland Strait.

By Bob Dixon

Cape Tormentine is a small fishing village nestled in the southeast corner of New Brunswick. It was home to one of the ferries that used to transport trains and cars from the mainland to Borden, Prince Edward Island before the Canadian government sponsored the construction of the Confederation Bridge.

From as far back as I can remember, my parents owned a waterfront cottage at Cape Tormentine. Ours was one of eleven or twelve cottages that lined the shoreline between the Cape Tormentine ferry dock and the lighthouse at Cape Jourimain, which also sits on the New Brunswick side about four kilometers northwest of the dock. On a clear day we could see the green hills of PEI rising up over the water some fourteen kilometers away.

The cottage was where our family whiled away the summer months. For a time during my youth, we were lucky enough to own three sloops, two outboard motorboats, and a dinghy, which my father moored behind a breakwater that he had built during the 1950s. We often went motorboating or sailing on the Northumberland Strait, sometimes travelling as far as Shediac, a coastal town seventy-two kilometers to the northwest, and quite often to Prince Edward Island. We were never afraid of sailing dangerously close to an approaching ferry because we knew that sailboats had the right of way, and on more than one occasion we forced the old Abegweit ferry off course.

I was always up to something with my friends from the nearby cottages. One day, when we were all in our mid-teens, four of us got together and decided to undertake a rather adventurous plan. We were all pretty good water-skiers, so we figured we would try water-skiing thirty kilometers across Northumberland Strait to Summerside. We packed a lunch, put on life jackets, and gassed up the boat. Jim wanted to drive, so Mac was the designated lookout for the narrow passage leading to the Summerside wharf. Hal and I were on water skis. Jim aimed the boat to where we thought Summerside should be, and we took off at full speed without permission from my parents because I knew they would say no.

The trip went fine for the first while, but about two thirds of the way across, I looked to my left and saw that Hal wasn't there anymore. He had fallen and no one had noticed.

We had made no plans for those in the boat to keep a watch on the skiers. Since the two in the boat were looking ahead, I began to shake the bar in my hands to make the towline oscillate, hoping that the reverberations of the rope would attract their attention. This went on for several minutes until Mac turned around and noticed immediately that Hal was missing. By that time we were so far away from the scene of the mishap that he was completely out of sight.

Now, in addition to lots of jellyfish, the Northumberland Straight has a fairly powerful tidal current, which means that when someone falls into the water they are soon far from the place where they fell. In our case, we didn't even know where Hal had fallen, or for that matter, in what direction the tidal current was flowing.

Jim swung the boat around and headed back in the general direction from which we had come. Luck was with us: about fifteen minutes later, we saw a worried Hal bobbing in the water. Jim turned again to bring the bar on the end of the rope as close to Hal as he could. Hal swam to the bar, we resumed the proper position, and we were soon on our way to the Summerside wharf again.

Upon our return to Cape Tormentine, Jim announced that we had run out of gas just as we hit the sandbar. Then it dawned on me: I had forgotten to calculate the amount of gas we would need to get to Summerside and back!

It wasn't long after that my older brother and his girlfriend, along with me and my brother's friend Todd, decided to play night-time hide-and-seek on the water in front of our cottage. We pulled out from behind the breakwater in our boats, armed with nothing more than flashlights and lanterns. One person was to drive off, stop the boat in a place unknown, then turn off the engine and the lights. When the boat that was seeking approached the hidden boat, the person in the hidden boat was to turn on his lights to indicate that the seeker was getting too close. It was decided that Todd and I would be the first to go and hide.

After we had stopped and turned off our lights, my brother and his girlfriend began searching for us. He accelerated his boat up to maximum speed and we watched him circle around fruitlessly for several minutes. Todd and I were sitting at opposite ends of the boat when, to our surprise, my brother turned in the dark and headed directly for us, aiming dead center at our starboard side.

As he approached, I turned on my lantern on to warn him of the impending crash. Unfortunately, the head of the lantern was on a swivel, and distracted by the oncoming boat, I didn't notice that the swivel was aiming the light directly at the floorboards. My brother couldn't see a thing.

As the bow of his speedboat rammed the side of ours, the force of impact lifted his boat out of the water. I watched with dismay as the dark form of his boat flew through the air between Todd and me—a mere foot from my face—and splashed into the water on the other side. I can still see the dark outline of the outboard motor as it passed in front of my eyes.

Miraculously, there were no injuries and no damage to his boat. Mine sustained some damage to the starboard side, but I was able to make it back to the dock.

When we got back to the cottage to inform our father of the incident, we expected to be severely reprimanded. It seemed quite strange to me that he wasn't angry, and that he actually seemed quite jovial about the entire affair. I understood why when the next day we had a boat-burning party and Dad collected on the insurance.

Today, the breakwater is virtually washed away. My older brother has just turned seventy, and my cottage friends and I are now in our sixties. Often we reminisce about these and other stories, like the day two friends and I were sailing a small sloop.

We had been swamped in shallow water over a sandbar by a gust of wind, but we were a half-mile from shore. When I dropped anchor to stabilize the boat, I discovered that the other end of the rope was not attached to the boat. The water between us and the shore was too deep to walk the boat in, so we had to wait for two hours, standing and holding the boat in four feet of water, until someone noticed that we were in difficulty and came to our rescue. If you happen to be walking along the sand flats at low tide, not far from the Cape Jourimain lighthouse, you might still come across our rusty old anchor.

The Dixon family cottage was built in the late 1940s and is now owned by the son-in-law of Bob's oldest brother. He and his wife now rent it out as a luxury summer vacation home. The breakwater has since washed away so there are no more boats. This is Bob Dixon's first story for a Summit Studios anthology.

Blue Window Van

Sometimes you catch fish in the darndest of places.

By Barbara McAlear

My three-year-old grandson Steven had recently discovered the sport of fishing, but this weekend he hadn't caught anything. He had spent many hours casting off the end of our pier, but to no avail. Not a single bite. Not even a nibble.

We had been staying at our Georgian Bay cottage on Christian Island for the weekend. Most of our family was there: Steven's mom and dad, his sister, his aunt and uncle, and their baby daughter. My husband and I had enjoyed our family time—though it always seemed to include a couple of wet dogs—and now we were on our way home, stuffed into our extended blue window van, tired but content.

But Steven was cranky. He was an energetic boy and could be short-tempered on road trips at the best of times. Now, given his lack of fishing success, he was quickly becoming inconsolable.

His grumpiness began wearing thin on the rest of us, but no matter what tactics we tried, we couldn't settle him down. We even tried singing "Ninety-nine Bottles of Beer on the Wall," which eventually got annoying because he couldn't count.

His fishing rod happened to be in the van, so we gave it to him and encouraged him to try his luck. Maybe there was a fish lurking somewhere inside the van. He looked skeptical, but began waving the rod around in the air, pretending that he was casting and reeling.

He was pretending to reel his fishing line in when, lo and behold, a fish appeared on his line!

Steven was stunned. We were stunned. He began trembling all over and yelling at the top of his lungs: "Look what I caught! Mommy, Gramma, Daddy … LOOK!" His eyes could not have been any wider.

Sitting in the seat behind him was his father, Glen. Unbeknownst to everyone else, Glen had reached into the cooler and attached a fish that we had purchased earlier that day from some neighbors.

As we looked at each other we tried very hard not to laugh. Everyone did their best to feign genuine amazement. "What a clever boy! Wow, look at that! I can't believe it! Steven, you must be magic!"

Steven was quiet the rest of the way home. His fish languished on his lap, sprawled over some newspaper, and he often reached down to stroke the fish along its side with a most amazed and proud look on his face.

For months after the fact, he would tell anyone who would listen about the "huge fish" he had caught in Grandpa's Blue Window Van. And although he loved to ride in that van ever after, he never asked to try his luck again.

Barbara McAlear's family no longer owns the cottage on Christian Island, but they remember fondly the many family gatherings at their "home away from home." Steven is now a 25-year-old chef. It has been many years since he tried fishing from inside a moving motor vehicle.

Two Sweaty Canadians

Catch me if you can.

By Andrew Shutsa

After five long years at university, I knew the "logical" thing to do was to look for an apartment, get a well-paying job in my field of interest, and start saving for the future.

I decided to call this Plan B.

During my tenure as a student at four different universities (and by that I mean bouncing around and not making up my mind about anything), I recall a lot of in-lecture laptop solitaire games, in-lecture napping, and I suppose a few actual in-lecture lectures. One that stuck with me was in a second-year history class.

After the professor—who I always thought looked like Frasier Crane—had gotten off-topic for the ninth time that class, we found ourselves discussing work opportunities and volunteer programs abroad. My professor said that as a teen he had participated in Canada World Youth, a program that matches young Canadians with young participants from other countries. They are put together in small teams and the teams take turns living and working in both countries.

Fast-forward three years: two diplomas and a few haircuts later, I was on an airplane headed for Ecuador. I had spent the last three and half months living and working with a Bolivian in small-town Alberta.

For the Ecuador phase, I was paired with Jeremy, a guy from Edmonton who shared my zany sense of humor. Jeremy and I were placed with a wonderful Quechua woman named Zoila and her grandson Paul (pronounced similar to Raul). She ran a small farm and owned a clothing shop and market booth in a nearby city.

Jeremy and I were excited to learn more Spanish and to experience firsthand the South American way of life. Working in the market was always fun, because as young men who looked like tourists, people would often try to sell us things, when in reality, we were there to sell *them* things.

Our favorite task, though, was on the farm. We often had to walk Zoila's two cows halfway up a nearby volcano to the grazing grounds that she owned. It was a bit of a trek, but we enjoyed it for many reasons: the exercise, the chance to chat on all subjects, and the opportunity to speak with local farmers. The scenery was absolutely spectacular, and we got to know that path very well.

At the end of one particularly hot day, we were coming down from the volcano when we saw Zoila's neighbor running up the path towards us, yelling, "Gringos!"

Jeremy's Spanish was far superior to mine, so she started describing something to him. (Jeremy was a Franco-Albertan, and his French language skills made it easier for him to pick up Spanish.) Nevertheless, I knew enough that I was starting to get the gist of what the neighbor was saying. Zoila's dog had apparently run up the hill behind our house, and she and Raul were not home to retrieve it.

Zoila had recently adopted the very pregnant dog. We were unsure as to the details of the transaction, but from what we gathered, she had gotten it from a friend who just wanted one of the dog's puppies in exchange.

We both looked up to where the neighbor was pointing. Sure enough, at the top of Zoila's garden and walking up the hill that ran back from her house, was the dog.

Jeremy started hiking up the hill, thinking it would be an easy task to retrieve the dog. We figured that in five minutes we would be back in the house, dog beside us, getting ready for an important group meeting in the town's square later that hour.

Jeremy hiked up … and so did the dog. Every time Jeremy made progress, the dog would speed up and pull herself out of reach again.

All right—Jeremy needed backup. I would have to get involved, and I was quite prepared to be the Robin to his Batman, the Kato to his Green Hornet.

I wouldn't describe the incline behind the house as a mountain by any means, but it was certainly a hill to be reckoned with. I started up after Jeremy, but he was soon out of sight. Moments later, I crested a major bump in the hill and saw Jeremy and the dog. There was still some distance between them.

At this point, Jeremy and I were sweating like professional athletes as we gained elevation rapidly, cutting across fields on the hillside. I took a field to the right while Jeremy took one to the left and we continued treading upwards. Thankfully we were in an area without any crops.

We made our way up to the second crest, still chasing the dog. We were now above several fields, looking over the farming area. One farmer saw the dog with two sweaty guys chasing it, and quickly put two and two together. Realizing that we could cut down on time by quickly running through his living room to the other side of the house, he promptly waved us in through his home. We ran through the kind stranger's living room, soaked in sweat, smiling and saying *"Hola!"* to as many dinner-eating family members as we could before we were back outside chasing the dog.

Jeremy and I were starting to get worried, as the sun was setting quickly and the dog was running like Leonardo DiCaprio in *Catch Me if You Can*—which I supposed would have made us Tom Hanks, so that put me in a good mood. (I'm a big fan of *Turner and Hooch*.)

Another stranger pointed behind his house, and there was the dog. The reason we were able to spot it was because we were now on an incline, descending the other side of the hill. I wouldn't say it was the edge of a cliff, but it was a dangerously steep drop that would be impossible to get footing on without proper equipment. The dog had reached a dead end. It would have been almost impossible for her to negotiate the steep drop-off, and Jeremy and I were legitimately concerned for her safety.

That's when the unexpected happened: she walked straight for Jeremy and sat down.

After a huge sigh of relief and an obligatory high five, we knew all we had to do was lead her home, which was about a fifteen-minute walk downhill. This time, we would be able to go in a straight line as opposed to crisscrossing the slopes several times.

This plan quickly changed, however, as the dog did not move. She sat at our feet and refused to move an inch. That settled it. How do you debate with a dog—especially a Spanish-speaking dog? So we picked her up and carried her down.

Jeremy and I traded off, carrying her down the hill. Every few minutes we tired out and handed her over to the other person. By the time we got to the bottom of the hill we were exhausted. But we felt good about ourselves; we'd retrieved the dog and brought her back safely. Perhaps there was a made-for-television movie in the works.

It was now 7:30 p.m. and we had been working all day. We had walked the cows up the volcano and back, then chased the dog up the hill and carried her back. However, if we didn't leave at that moment, we would've been late for our group meeting. As a result, we had no choice but to leave in our work clothes with a less-than-flattering smell.

When we spoke to Zoila that evening, we found out that she had arrived back at the house ten minutes after we dropped the dog off, and that within a few minutes of her return home, the dog had started to give birth. It seemed reasonable that her escapade up the hill was her way of looking for a quiet place to have her babies. That evening, seven puppies were sleeping in the back of Zoila's house—six of which are still alive and well today. All of them are named Paul after her grandson. Some would say the naming system is just a four-year-old being silly; I say it's efficient.

Andrew had a great time backpacking around South America, but now lives in Seoul, South Korea where he works as a grade five teacher at a Canadian international school. He currently works out by lifting free-weights as opposed to free-dogs.

A Paynes Christmas

In pursuit of Yuletide sushi at a climbers' campground in New Zealand.

By Michael Hall

Perhaps it was the absence of blinding snowstorms, consumerist jingles, flashing lights, frantic shoppers, traffic jams, and bad Touchstone/Disney films that allowed me to sidestep gut-wrenching nostalgia for my first Christmas away from Canada. Then again, maybe it was waking up in a tent, being concerned about sunburn rather than frostbite, eating out of the same pot for weeks, and getting water from a tap in the bushes.

It can hardly be called Christmas when there's always somebody playing Bob Marley on a guitar and you fall asleep to the sounds of camp hooligans throwing gas canisters on the fire. (You never get used to those explosions!)

It was Christmas Eve at the Hangdog rock climber's campground at Paynes Ford, New Zealand, which is located at the northern tip of the South Island. Together with my friends Steve and Monica, I had decided that sitting around a graveyard of candles in down jackets is just too much of a climber's cliché. So in pitch darkness we stumbled to a nearby swimming hole to drink cheap beer and howl at the moon.

Shortly after arriving we discovered that the rumors were true: Feral Dan *had* found a large, dead pukeko bird on the highway, and had attached the bird to the end of a hanging rope to attract eels. The bird's bloated carcass bobbed on the surface of the water.

Sufficiently disgusted, we sat on the limestone shelf and watched the moon paint a silver veneer on the surface of the silent river. We talked about past climbing adventures and dreamed of destinations for the future.

After a while, our attention turned back to the dead pukeko bird.

"Hunting eels is a pretty boring business," said Steve.

"Yep," I agreed as I finished the last of my cheap New Zealand beer. I crushed the can under my foot and stuffed it into my pocket. "But it's safe to say we've never had a Christmas Eve quite like this one."

I got down on my stomach and leaned over the water to get a good look at the bloated mass of feathers. As my eyes adjusted to the neon blue of my headlamp, I saw a snakelike movement below the surface of the water.

"Holy crap! There's an eel!"

Suddenly Steve and Monica were beside me, our trio of headlamps illuminating a feeding frenzy.

"Another one!"

"Look at that one!"

Sure enough, the mother eel had arrived for a feast of pukeko. She was at least three feet long and as wide as my arm. Her luminescent eyes glowed like tiny televisions as she stalked her prey. Chills jangled my spine.

"We have to catch it!" shrieked Monica. "We'll be heroes back at the camp. We can cook it up and serve Christmas eel to everyone!"

"What a wonderful idea," I replied. "And just how do you propose we do that? These things are very slippery."

"Can you just grab it with your hands?"

"Just grab it with my hands?" It sounded like an ill-fated suggestion if there ever was one, but for some reason I positioned myself leaning far over the edge and reached out over the water. My fingers dipped below the surface and caressed the eel's smooth back.

"I touched it!"

"Not only that!" shouted Steve. "It didn't even care that you touched it! Can you grab it?"

"Okay. So let's say I *can* grab it and pull it out. Then what?"

"I'll smack it with the axe?" Steve suggested.

"Might work."

Steve grabbed the campsite's "eeling axe" from under the bench. I took a deep breath and tried to visualize how much strength I would need to grab that slimy creature and pull it out of the water.

When I finally grabbed it, the eel was heavier than I had expected. I applied my rock-climbing grip and pulled hard. The eel breached and started convulsing frantically as Steve came at it with the axe. Then the eel latched its merciless fangs on to the soft flesh of my cheek and I lost my balance. For a moment it was me that was flailing, before I fell screaming into the river with an angry eel attached to my face.

I awoke from this terrible reverie with my hands hesitating over the beast. My body felt cold. The eel, with a good-sized piece of pukeko in its fangs, suddenly did a violent roll.

"Ahhh!" shouted Monica. "A death roll!"

Then, at the most opportune moment, the Maori gods from Golden Bay mercifully intervened. Headlamps appeared behind us, signaling the arrival of beer and Hangdog camp residents who had actual experience hunting eels.

Seven of us spent the next hour on our bellies staring down at the drama a few inches below the surface. We duct-taped a steak knife onto a broom handle, and hidden in darkness, we stalked our fearsome quarry.

Despite our best efforts, we took no eel home that night. For when the moment of truth arrived, the spear snapped, and like some divine message from above, the vaporous walls that had enfolded us suddenly evaporated. The eel, sensing that it had become the prey, disappeared into some dark hole, its fate as backwoods sushi averted for yet another day.

The half-drunk climbers, tired and finished with the business of eeling, stumbled home with a broken spear, an axe, and pockets full of crushed empties. And the pukeko? Well, it remained tied to the rope, none of us quite sure what to do with the dead, bloated bird at 2:00 a.m. on Christmas morning.

Mercifully, there was no screaming and yelling that night, no exploding gas bombs or chants of "BURN THE COUCH! BURN THE COUCH!" We slept like babies all night long, and after enjoying some difficult Christmas Day climbs and a long lay in the field to let the cows lick salt off our backs, we headed to the swimming hole to cool off. We were all relieved that the pukeko had disappeared.

From what I've been told, this was just a regular Paynes Christmas.

Michael J.P. Hall is a writer, photographer and explorer based in Vancouver. Accounts of his adventures have been published in a variety of international magazines, including The Globe & Mail, Climbing, *and* Rock & Ice *magazines. You can find him in cyberspace at **www.michaeljphall.com**.*

The Hippie Commune

It's, like, groovy man!

By Russell Jennings

It was midafternoon and I was eighty kilometers north of San Francisco, standing on the shoulder of Interstate 5 trying to hitch a ride north.

In the midst of a steady stream of vehicles, a van slowed down and stopped. It was a '53 Chevy, painted in psychedelic colors from bumper to bumper. Portraits of grotesque monsters swirled in hues of purple, yellow, red, blue, and green.

I pulled open the passenger door and shot a nervous glance at the driver, a thickset man in his twenties dressed in a flowery Hawaiian shirt. He wore his long brown hair tied in a ponytail. I thanked him for stopping, heaved my backpack onto the floor on the passenger side, and hoisted myself into the seat.

Someone coughed behind me. I turned. Three guys in their twenties greeted me with a collective "Hi, man."

As the miles rolled beneath the wheels, I got to know something of our driver, Alan. Originally from Rhode Island, he had come to the West Coast to find what he called "action." He now lived in a house in Seattle, which he shared with about twenty adults and four children living a communal lifestyle.

"We want to be self-supporting," he told me, "so we run a candle-making business in the basement of the house. We want to remain outside mainstream society as much as possible, but it's not easy. The rural communes that grow their own food have an easier time sustaining themselves."

"Sounds like an interesting place," I said, genuinely intrigued. "I've never experienced communal living before."

After two hours of driving, Alan suggested we all chip in some money to buy food for a picnic dinner. When we all agreed, Alan took the exit ramp into Redding.

It was a motley crew that exited from the van at a mini-supermarket. With the exception of Alan, all were wanderers who had been hitchhiking together on Interstate 5.

The first guy out of the back of the van was dressed in frayed blue jeans and a purple, tie-dyed T-shirt. He wore a black dog collar around his neck, complete with chromed rivets.

Next came a sallow-cheeked man who didn't look very healthy. His wild blond hair and scraggly beard hadn't seen scissors for months. He wore Chinese peasants' trousers and an oversized green shirt that draped loosely over his skinny frame.

The third to emerge was a man with fair hair, freckles, and steel-rimmed glasses. He appeared nervous and scratched constantly at his rib cage.

With my short hair, trim beard and relatively neat clothes, I was the oddity in this group.

In the mini-supermarket we bought bread, cold cuts of corned beef, lettuce, carrots, a jar of coleslaw, and a carton of milk—

healthy enough choices, it seemed to me. We climbed into the van and drove until we found a picnic table in a park, where we prepared and munched on sandwiches.

"Where are you guys heading?" I asked the three other passengers.

"Oregon," said the skinny one. "We're going to pick shrooms."

"Shrooms?"

"Mushrooms. The magic kind."

"What makes them magic?"

"Something in them gives you a sort of out-of-body experience. Makes you feel like you're dreaming when you're actually awake. A bit like being on LSD."

"Taking that sort of stuff doesn't appeal to me," I said. "I like my two feet firmly on the ground. What happens if you eat too many shrooms?"

"You could die, man. There are two kinds of magic mushroom eaters—the smart ones and the dead ones. Even some of the smart ones are now dead. At least mushrooms aren't addictive; you can stop eating them whenever you want to. But there are side effects. They can make you nervous. And they can give you itchy skin."

The sun, which had been shining warmly, retreated under thick clouds. A cold wind whipped at our clothes. It was time to move on. The freckled guy with glasses continued to scratch himself.

The three shroom pickers left us in Oregon, and because Alan was eager to drive through the night, he and I shared time behind the wheel. I learned more about Alan. He put all his energy into the candle business and occasionally suffered fits of depression.

His commune colleagues had encouraged him to borrow the commune's van and go on a holiday. After spending two weeks on California's beaches, he was now anxious to return to Seattle.

We took turns napping and driving. After a pre-dawn nap, I watched the sky begin to lighten. Alan estimated we would arrive in Seattle at three in the afternoon, and he invited me to stay overnight.

I said yes, but suddenly I had misgivings. Would I be accepted by the other commune members, whose lifestyle, I imagined, was so different from my own? I had heard about the counterculture's loose sleeping arrangements, drugs, strict vegetarianism, aversion to work, and distrust of anyone over thirty. I was twenty-eight, so surely my age would not be held against me. The presence of drugs bothered me, but I would just decline if somebody offered me something.

The communal house was a ramshackle wooden building with three stories, obviously built long ago. It was white with dark blue trim around the door and window frames. The roof was threadbare and the windows were streaked with dirt.

Alan showed me around the house. The main floor included a kitchen and a dining room with oak floorboards that squeaked. All the other rooms were bedrooms; even the attic space was divided into bedrooms. The basement was used solely for the manufacture of candles.

Alan appeared to be the leader of the commune, although he wouldn't admit it. He asked me not to divulge the address of the house to anyone. "We're renting the house," he told me, "and we don't want the owner to know we are making candles in the basement. We use a lot of wax, which is a fire hazard."

Half a dozen of the commune members were going to another commune house for a twenty-first birthday party that evening, and Alan invited me to join them. At nine-thirty, our small group set out to walk the six blocks to the other commune. After ambling along a residential street of houses that ranged from mildly neglected to decrepit, we arrived at the commune, another three-story house in very poor shape. The sounds from an old Bob Dylan record pulsated through windows that were partly covered with old plastic wrap, no doubt to stop winter's chilly winds from blowing through the gaps in the window frames.

The group climbed the front steps to the main floor and someone rapped on the door before pushing it open. We headed toward the music along a gloomy hallway with carpet that smelled of cats and mildew, and then entered a living room packed with forty or so hippies. The men sported tie-dyed T-shirts, beaded necklaces, loose cotton trousers, and sandals; the women wore long dresses of Indian cotton, silver anklets, and beaded necklaces.

Toward eleven o'clock, someone announced a toast to the birthday boy and everyone was handed a glass of champagne. As people drank their bubbly, they started to drop like flies onto the floor.

I suddenly felt a wave of fuzziness in my brain, and I also collapsed. Monsters with bright psychedelic colors swirled in my mind, not unlike the ones painted on Alan's van. It took me over two hours to return to some form of normality. It wasn't something that I would ever want to experience again.

Alan, livid that someone had spiked the champagne with a hallucinatory drug, mustered our group. Someone said the drug was Orange Sunshine, a form of LSD.

"That stuff's powerful," said Alan. "These guys probably put a microdot of it in each champagne bottle."

We started back, albeit somewhat unsteadily, to our house. A gentle, misty rain fell. I couldn't feel it, but I could see it as we ambled happily from one halo of light to another. A cone of illuminated drops spilled beneath each street lamp. It looked as if the lamps themselves were raining.

At the house, Alan suggested I sleep in a corner of the dining room. From somewhere he produced a foam mattress to make the few remaining hours before dawn comfortable.

Morning arrived early for me with a sound like the crack of a whip. I opened an eye and saw bare legs stride past me. A second whip crack sounded, accompanied by loud squeaks. Realizing that the old oak floor was responding to the weight of the footsteps, I opened my other eye to see who the intruder was and glimpsed the back of a tall, thin woman. A tumble of fiery red curls cascaded down her back, ending at her bare buttocks.

Now my eyes were wide open. The woman turned to enter the kitchen, displaying a generous bust. I heard cupboards and drawers being opened and closed noisily. She was probably in search of breakfast.

I rolled over and tried to go back to sleep, but that wasn't to be. The floorboards creaked again as she retraced her steps past my corner of the room and disappeared down the hall.

I dragged myself out of my sleeping bag and padded to the kitchen to investigate the food supply; I discovered plastic containers of caraway seeds, peanuts and soy nuts. Was this what hippies lived on? I felt like an alien. I delved into my backpack and found a couple of granola bars—my survival rations—and ate them for breakfast.

Hearing noises from the basement workshop, I walked downstairs and found Alan supervising students who had come to pour candles. The smell of wax hung heavily in the air.

"We pay them five dollars an hour," he told me. "The candles are thirty-six inches long. To make a candle, we hang a wick on a nail and attach a half-pound lead weight to the bottom to keep the wick taut. We heat paraffin in a five-gallon tin to 110 degrees Celsius, or 230 degrees Fahrenheit, on the electric stove, and then add wax hardener, dye and scents. A worker dips a tin coffee pot into the mixture and gently pours the wax down the wick. This will be repeated fifty or sixty times until the thirty-six-inch taper has a diameter of one inch at the base.

"We're getting orders from New York and San Francisco," he continued. "A problem we have is how to wrap and pack the candles so they won't chafe and lose their sheen in transit. We're still looking for a solution."

Someone called out, "Lunch in fifteen minutes." I thought of caraway seeds and peanuts. Lunch would be interesting.

I headed upstairs to the dining room and walked in on a roundtable discussion about seeds and herbs. I wondered if they were talking about the lunch menu, and it occurred to me that they might be surprised if I mentioned the supermarket food Alan had eaten for dinner the previous night.

One man's discourse was interrupted by what sounded like a pistol shot—the old floor again! As people walked across it, the floorboards protested with loud cracks and squeaks. I glanced up to see the woman with the fiery red hair. This time she wore a dark green Indian cotton skirt and blouse. A young girl and boy clung to her legs.

I was the only stranger in the room. The redhead introduced herself as Shea and added, "These are my twins, Fiare Genie and One Free. They're six years old."

One Free was a freckle-faced boy with copper-brown hair. Fiare had inherited her mother's red hair; it was tied in double ponytails placed high on her head so that they looked like puppy ears. Apparently, two other children named Ocean and Skye lived in the commune, but they were away with their parents, picking magic mushrooms.

There was a commotion at the dining room door. "Here comes lunch!" someone shouted, piquing my interest.

I turned to see three of the hippies carrying milk, a large jar of coleslaw, a big paper bag overflowing with french fries ... and two huge cardboard buckets of Colonel Sanders' Kentucky Fried Chicken!

Russell Jennings connected with his wife Penny on a blind date in 1975. Since then, they have left their sandal prints in dozens of countries on six continents. Russell is the author of Around the World in Sandals, *a collection of stories and amusing anecdotes about their many round-the-world journeys. More recently he released* Timbuktu, where are you? *another collection of stories from which this one was selected and adapted. You can find Russell and Penny online at* **www.worldweatherguide.com**.

Drake and the Ducks

Birds of a feather stick together.

By Janice Sabulsky

"Ducks! Baby ducks!" said the breathless voice on the other end of the telephone.

I held the receiver a couple of inches away from my ear and asked, "Sharon, is that you?"

Without acknowledging my question, Sharon continued her tirade. "I think a cat must have got the mother. I'm following them all over the place. I'll call you later."

The one-way conversation ended abruptly. On my scale of unusual occurrences, this was not even on my radar. I poured myself a cup of coffee and surveyed my rescue sanctuary. The doves were cooing softly and the canaries were taking their first bath of the day. The new cockatiel seemed to be settling in with the others. Life was good.

I guess a little background is in order. I live with my husband Leo in Chetwynd, British Columbia, and am known locally as the "Bird Lady." Sometimes people use the word "crazy" in front of that title.

My love affair with birds started innocently enough when I took home a partly paralyzed diamond dove from the local pet store. I built handicapped steps for it so that it could access its perch, and over the next year I began taking other birds from the pet store that were sick or injured. Word got out that I would take injured birds and soon there was a steady stream of them arriving on my doorstep from people who didn't want them anymore.

Sharon was often my "adoption broker." Sometimes people brought their birds over to my house to look after when they went on vacation and never bothered to pick them up again. At any given time I might have seventy or eighty birds in my house—which I now call Simon House, after the first diamond dove I rescued.

It does get a bit noisy in the summer when the sun comes up at 3:30 a.m., but that's why blinds were invented. Some of the birds also harass my husband and our dog Romeo. They've become experts at sounding like the fire pager (my husband is the fire chief) and when it goes off there are several dozen birds that can mimic the sound. It's absolute chaos.

One of the birds has also learned to mimic my husband's voice and sometimes calls out, "Romeo! Romeo!" Our dog runs around in circles, barking and searching for my husband who may or may not be at home at the time.

Back to the story of the ducks. Late in the afternoon, the phone rang again. "You gotta come to Mike's place. You know where Mike the plumber lives, right?" *Click.* One of these days she's going to get a wrong number. Would she even realize it?

I arrived at the property to see three people crouching on the ground as if preparing for a missile attack.

"So," I asked, "what are we looking for?"

As I spoke, they bolted upright and started shouting. I saw a fluffy ball supported by two legs dash under a pickup truck.

"Baby ducks," said Sharon. "Remember?"

I could tell by her tone that she had stopped just short of adding "Duh!" to her answer. I was somewhat grateful for that.

Over the next thirty minutes, the four of us chased, herded, and collected five fuzzy ducklings and put them into a plastic critter keeper.

"I've been following them all day," said Sharon. "There's no sign of the mother. It's getting dark and I'm scared a cat will get them. Here you go."

In one smooth motion, she thrust the box into my hands and turned quickly in the direction of her house. I watched her retreat, her skirt fluttering around her legs and her sandals slapping on her heels.

I turned to speak to the others. They had also vanished.

I looked suspiciously in the direction of Mike's house. I could picture Mike and his friend hiding behind the couch, motioning each other to keep quiet.

At home, I found one of the many birdcages I had stored in the garage, hastily grabbed a water tin, and picked fresh grass for bedding. I placed the ducks in the cage, set the cage on the deck, and studied the ducklings. They were far from ugly. Indeed, they were beautiful!

But that feeling of elation quickly evaporated as the first wave of panic hit me. What could I feed them? My only information on ducks involved a Maggie Muggins story my mother had read to me years before. The duck was named Cornmeal Katie.

Seizing on that one word—cornmeal—I mixed up some cornmeal mash and put it into the cage. The ducks ignored it completely and snuggled in the opposite corner.

The next morning, I rushed out onto the deck to check on my new adoptees. The water bowl was turned over. The cornmeal mash had dried and was sticking to their feathers. They looked like tiny Sputniks with irregular yellow balls protruding from their backsides.

Perhaps a large bowl of water would help them feel more at home—or at least get rid of the Sputnik effect. I emptied the big silver bowl that contained the dog's water, cleaned it, and refilled it with warm water. As I reached to place the first duckling into the water, Romeo appeared at my elbow with an accusatory glare. Ignoring him, I quickly placed the ducks into the bowl.

Just as I was about to congratulate myself for my act of genius, I realized that something was very wrong. The sounds coming from the bowl resembled liquid being mixed in a blender. The ducks hated being in the water, and their tiny feet were turning like eggbeaters! I quickly pulled them out and dried them with a tea towel.

Later that morning I returned from the local feed store clutching a bag of chick starter. I rigged up a wire to secure the water tin to the side on the cage. One duck bustled up to the feed dish, dove in, and started eating the food. The others followed shortly thereafter. I felt triumphant.

Over the next few days they continued to rush around the cage and jump in and out of the water dish. I watched them snuggle with each other and I stroked their soft down coats with my fingers. They were absolutely beautiful.

It soon became apparent that one of the ducks was the leader. When the brood slept, he was always awake, keeping watch. He always tested the water and took the first bite of food before the rest joined in. I decided to name him Drake.

Near the end of the first week I found one of the ducklings huddled in the far corner of the cage. His head was down and his eyes were only partially open. A swell of panic rose in my chest. Maybe the food I'd been giving them was no good after all. Did the misguided bath I gave them cause pneumonia? I carefully put the ailing duck back with the others. I reasoned that they would keep him warm and comfort him.

When I returned home several hours later, I found the little guy back in the corner, barely breathing. I wrapped him up in a washcloth, dribbled some water into his bill and held him close to my chest. I knew what was coming. More than anything, I hated feeling powerless. He gave a little shudder and went limp. I placed him in a shoebox and stared anxiously at the other four.

When I woke the next morning I realized that something strange had happened overnight: the cage had shrunk to half its original size. The ducks could barely turn around without hitting the sides. It was time for an upgrade. I enlisted the help of my son, who rushed over with a large rabbit cage.

I placed a wide, shallow flowerpot into the cage as a water container. Within minutes, the ducklings had tipped it over. I was starting to feel like the parent of an unpredictable adolescent.

Later, I returned to the cage and found the ducks curled up and sleeping inside the flowerpot, basking in the warm sunlight. Drake was looking around like a watchful sentinel. His brown eyes looked at me steadily. He probably thinks I'm pathetic, I thought. These ducklings are thriving in spite of my efforts.

It wasn't long before the rabbit cage became cramped. I dragged out an old vinyl playpen from the garage, put it on the deck, and set the dog's water bowl into the depression. Victory was mine—I had created an enclosure with a built-in pool.

Romeo hung his long ears over the edge of the playpen. Drake lunged at him and he retreated with his head buried under a chair cushion.

Within two weeks, the playpen became stretched to the limit. The ducks were growing and becoming upwardly mobile. Their downy covering was being replaced by beautiful, sleek feathers. Cleaning the enclosure was also becoming more of a problem. What had previously been accomplished with paper towel now required a small shovel.

For the next phase of the housing crisis, I enlisted the help of my husband. He lit his pipe, walked away muttering, and returned within minutes with a huge wooden playpen. We carried the ducks onto the lawn, flipped the playpen upside down, put it over them, and watched them explore the soft grass.

Later that night, as the sun was setting, I sat in a lawn chair enjoying their company. It was then that I realized I was no longer their protector. I had become their captor.

Several days later—and eleven weeks after I had first taken the ducklings home—my husband and I crammed them into the old rabbit cage and headed for a pond. I held the cage on my lap as we drove and felt a tear sliding down my cheek. Was I about to make the biggest mistake of my life? Would they survive and know what to do without having their food dish filled all day long? Would the other ducks in the lake bully them?

We walked to the edge of the pond and set the cage down. Neither of us wanted to make the first move. Finally, I opened the cage and stepped back.

Nothing happened.

Just as I was beginning to feel that familiar sensation of panic, Drake exited the cage and walked boldly to the edge of the water. He flew forward and alighted on the pond's surface, skating across the water like a skipping stone.

In unison, the others followed Drake's lead. I watched them with a familiar sense of joy and sadness. Like children, they had never really been ours to keep.

A week later we returned to the pond. I called and called for the ducks. At the far end of the lake we finally spotted Drake, marching proudly, the other three following behind him with an air of unbridled confidence.

Not wanting to relinquish the serenity of the pond, we sat on a couple of stumps and enjoyed the atmosphere. As I got up to leave, I caught a movement from the corner of my eye. I found myself staring into Drake's familiar, soft brown eyes. He remained beside me, looking at the others who were out in the pond, and then looked back at me. Then he walked back to edge of the pond and slipped gracefully into the water. Life was good for all of us.

Janice Sabulsky has been taking birds into her home for almost a decade; she presently has 65 birds under her care. A few years ago she began taking pictures of her birds and this led to the creation of five children's books, which include photos and stories about her flock. They are currently unpublished. "Drake and the Ducks" was initially written as a children's book so that she could share the story of the ducks with her four-year-old grandson Mateus.

Dispatches from the Edge

A collection of wacky anecdotes from the road less traveled.

Bears Beware

In the early 1970s, Gerald and Heather Hudson went hiking and camping for several days in northern British Columbia, Canada. During their second day—in a place that was miles from nowhere—they were following a trail along the shoreline of a small lake when they heard sounds from up ahead. A few moments later, they came into a clearing where two black bears were tearing through some backpacks and gorging themselves on the food inside.

The couple surmised that two paddlers had left their food unattended while portaging their canoe to the next lake. Worried the campers would lose all of their supplies, Gerald decided to scare the bears away.

There were two paddles leaning against a tree, so he grabbed one of them and started waving it wildly at the bears. The bruins—having probably seen dozens of canoeists—were suitably unimpressed. They ignored Gerald and continued eating. To get the bears' attention, Gerald tried beating the paddle against a nearby tree. Unfortunately, after a few smacks, the paddle broke in half.

The bears continued eating.

Determined to help his fellow campers, Gerald grabbed the second paddle and began shouting and dancing madly around the bears. He got as close as he felt safe and started smacking the paddle against a tree that was directly beside the bears ... which is when the second paddle broke.

Startled, Gerald turned and walked sheepishly back to where his wife Heather was hiding. "I think we should go," he said.

The canoeists no doubt returned sometime later to find their supplies eaten and their paddles—their only means of getting home—lying on the ground in splinters.

- Sarah Bonar

Room with a Spew

According to an Australian web site, a woman named Anne Anderson and her family traveled to Queensland, Australia for their holidays in 2005. One afternoon, as they sat having lunch in their sixteenth-floor hotel room—which featured a stunning view of Surfer's Paradise—they heard the sirens of a fire brigade coming down a nearby street. Curious, Anne and her mother rushed to the balcony for a closer look.

While the women admired the view—and searched for the source of the sirens—they laughed heartily and kibitzed back and forth. As Anne tells it, "We were laughing at something and it made my Mom 'splutter'."

The result of this "spluttering" was that her mother's false teeth popped out of her mouth and dropped over the balcony's edge. The two women watched with horror as the teeth fell the entire sixteen stories to the pool area, where they landed with a faint *thud.*

While her mother raced downstairs, Anne kept her eyes fixed on the location where the teeth had landed. Once in the pool area, her mother exchanged pleasantries with several tourists lounging at the pool, then rustled through the shrubbery and found her teeth nestled in a flowerbed—completely intact.

- Matt Jackson

The Mouthy Mouse

Diane Nicholson's father was an avid hunter and rugged outdoorsman, and as such, camping trips were a favorite activity for her family. One camping trip to British Columbia's Manning Provincial Park is particularly memorable.

The family arrived in the afternoon and pitched their canvas army tent beside a burbling creek, which was surrounded on all sides by mountains. Diane and her three siblings spent the evening playing in the woods, roasting marshmallows, and telling stories around the campfire. Everyone went to sleep content.

The next morning, the children woke to the famous mantra their father recited whenever he was shaving in front of the mirror: "Goddamn it, Sherwood, you are a handsome man!" He gently shook everyone awake, then started cooking a hearty camp breakfast. The kids were handed juice and cereal, and when the coffee water had boiled, Diane's father poured himself a large, steaming mug.

Seconds later, Diane heard a blood-curdling shriek. It had come from her mother, who was pointing at her father with a horrified look. Out of Sherwood's mouth was hanging an odd, stringy thing. Her father—whose face had turned bone-white—reached up and pulled out a dead mouse.

The mouse had climbed into the coffeepot overnight and, unable to climb out again, had drowned. The next morning, Sherwood had boiled the water for coffee without looking inside—and ended up with a rodent latte.

For the rest of the trip, at the mere mention of the coffeepot mouse, Diane's father had to pull off the highway and vomit.

- Diane Nicholson

Crooked Creek

Two brothers, Ross and Keith Johnson, make an annual hunting pilgrimage to a meandering waterway north of Thunder Bay, Ontario. Their primary target is moose. They paddle up the creek in their canoe, lifting the light watercraft over the many beaver dams that control the flow of the river.

One year, when the water was quite high, the beaver lodge near the lake had become a huge tenement structure and the supplies for the beaver colony's winter food stock were being dragged from a great way up the creek. As the Johnson brothers were returning from one of their early morning patrols, they overtook a beaver that was towing a large willow sapling downstream. The beaver was making good headway at a speed only a bit less than what the brothers could paddle, so they grabbed a branch and relaxed.

Occasionally a branch from the tree would become entangled with some driftwood or other obstacle in the creekbed, at which point the beaver would swim to the offending obstacle and get rid of it with a few snips of his incisors. As Keith likes to say, "Our little buck-toothed rickshaw driver delivered us to Number One Beaver Place free of charge."

It wasn't long after this incident that the beavers attempted "revenge."

Keith made his living climbing hydro poles, so he would sometimes use his spurs to scale a strategically placed tree in order to spot a moose. On one such occasion he had ensconced himself about fifty feet up in a white poplar tree, which overlooked a fairly open meadow near the creek. As he studied the terrain and listened intently for any clue to the possible approach of a moose, he was startled by a loud *cronch! cronch!* sound from directly below his perch. He looked down and, lo and behold, there was a beaver chewing at the very tree he was sitting in.

Johnson wasn't worried that he couldn't make his escape before the tree was felled, but he didn't want the beaver's gnawing to interfere with his listening process. With his jackknife he quietly pruned a sizeable limb from the tree and dropped it on the interloper. That interrupted the beaver's chewing only briefly. Two or three more sticks thrown down had similar effect.

That's when Johnson—a resourceful backcountry woodsman—had an idea. He twisted precariously around on the branch until he was facing outward. He then unzipped his pants and proceeded to pee on the beaver.

This plan proved to be very effective. The beaver immediately quit his project and shuffled off towards the creek. Johnson offers this as proof that scent marking of territorial boundaries is an effective behavioral code among animals.

- Keith Johnson

Hanging Around

In the fall of 2007, hydro workers from Bracebridge, Ontario were laying new power cables along the ground. The autumn, of course, is the time of year bull moose can get rather ornery and temperamental.

For some reason, one of the resident moose became agitated by the cables and began thrashing at them, getting his antlers tangled in the process. When the construction workers—who were several kilometers away—tried hoisting the lines up with their equipment, the moose went right up with them.

The workers quickly realized that something was amiss. They were puzzled by excess tension in the lines, so they went searching for the problem. What they found was a large bull moose hanging from their power lines—several meters off the ground—and still very much alive.

When they lowered him back to terra firma, he was more than a little peeved!

- Matt Jackson

Addicted to Fruit

After a pleasant day of sea kayaking along British Columbia's Sunshine Coast, Philip Torrens paddled up a side channel called Tzoonie Narrows at slack water. The next campsite was several kilometers away, so he was happy to discover the orchard of a long-abandoned homestead, where he decided to spend the night.

The tent was up and Philip was preparing to cook dinner when a movement on the opposite bank of the narrows caught his eye. Coming down the slope was a large black bear, and as Philip watched, the bear waded into the water and swam purposefully across the tidal river toward him.

Once ashore, the bear strode in businesslike fashion directly at Philip, who by this time was on his feet and nervously backing up to one side. Rather than alter his course, however, the bear continued walking straight through the campsite with the impatience of a mammal on a mission. He went straight to one of the apple trees and climbed it with his impressive claws. Then, with the practised skill of a lumberjack, the bear walked out along a branch and started bouncing up and down on it, which resulted in a hail of apples falling to the ground. After a couple of minutes the bear climbed back down to enjoy feasting on the fruits of his labor.

Over the next hour, Philip watched the bear gorge himself repeatedly. Like the veteran fruit picker he was, the bear would climb the tree to liberate more apples, and then climb back down to continue with his meal.

Eventually, the bear sought out a sunlit patch of grass for a well-earned nap. Seeing the bear lying on his side, it was clear to Philip that he was one prosperous bear, who hadn't missed any meals recently. Nevertheless, Philip wasn't convinced he could pass a restful night with the bear lying a few meters away. So he packed up camp and set off for the next campsite, which by this time didn't seem all that far away.

Bearly far enough, in fact.

- Philip Torrens

Do you have a Great Story?

If you enjoyed this collection of stories and feel you have an outrageous, funny, heartwarming or inspirational tale that you would like to share, we would love to hear from you. Our only rules are that your story has some unusual, illuminating or humorous twist to it, that it's a true anecdote, and that it has something to do with travel or the Great Outdoors.

We are already working on a sixth volume of our travel and outdoor humor series and we are willing to look at either story proposals or pieces that have already been written. You don't have to be a professional writer. We look forward to hearing from anybody that has a great yarn to spin.

To obtain more detailed submission guidelines, please visit Summit Studios on our web site at:

www.summitstudios.biz

Please submit stories or story proposals by e-mail, fax, or snail mail to:

SUMMIT STUDIOS
#105, 2572 Birch St.
Vancouver, BC V6H 2T4

E-mail: submissions@summitstudios.biz

We look forward to hearing from you.

Acknowledgements

A very special thanks to my wife, Stacey, who shares my passion for travel and the outdoors. She also shares my love for great stories. Without her unconditional support and her belief in my dream to found a publishing company, it would not have been possible to share these stories with you.

A big thanks to Curtis Foreman for his help with the copy editing and to Kirk Seton for a fantastic book design. They are both top-notch professionals.

Thanks to Pat Toth-Smith for the great cover image of the smiling bear.

I'm grateful to www.paddling.net for passing along the contact information of several writers who've contributed to their web site. Four stories in this anthology were adapted from tales that originally appeared on paddling.net.

Thanks to my friends and family members who have offered their ideas, support, and critical feedback as this book has taken shape.

And finally, thanks to the many travelers who have contributed their stories to this book. Their willingness to share means that we're all a little richer.

Other Titles by Matt Jackson

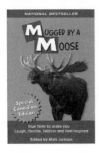

Mugged by a Moose

Edited by Matt Jackson

Is a bad day spent outside really better than a good day at the office? This collection of twenty-three short stories aims to answer that question.

> Humor/Travel • Softcover • 216 pages
> $19.95 • ISBN 9780973467130

Canadian Bestseller

"It's like Chicken Soup for the Funny Bone."
- *The Kitchener-Waterloo Record*

A Beaver is Eating My Canoe

Edited by Matt Jackson

Another collection of wacky, funny, and inspiring tales from the far side of beyond, written by twenty-five free-spirited wanderers.

> Humor/Travel • Softcover • 224 pages
> $19.95 • ISBN 9780973467161

The Canada Chronicles:
A Four-year Hitchhiking Odyssey

Written by Matt Jackson

Join the author on a four-year hitchhiking journey across Canada as he logs almost 30,000 kilometers, takes more than 25,000 photographs and meets hundreds of interesting characters from every corner of the country.

Adventure/Travel • Softcover
384 pages • 60 color photographs
$25.00 • ISBN 9780973467123

**Canadian Bestseller and Winner of the 2005 IPPY Award
for Best North American Travel Memoir!**

"Jackson's humor and charm shine throughout his storytelling."
- Canadian Geographic Magazine

A Bear Stole My Fishing Boat

Edited by Matt Jackson

Traveling is not for the timid of heart. What can go wrong often does, as twenty-six travel-hardened writers relate in this book.

Humor/Travel • Softcover • 216 pages
$19.95 • ISBN 9780973467178

About Matt Jackson

A graduate of Wilfrid Laurier's Business Administration program in Waterloo, Canada, Matt Jackson was lured away from the corporate world by the thrill of adventure journalism while still a university student. He is now an author, editor, photojournalist and professional speaker, and is the president of Summit Studios, a publishing company specializing in books about travel and the outdoors.

Matt's first book, *The Canada Chronicles: A Four-year Hitchhiking Odyssey*, is a Canadian bestseller and won the IPPY award for best North American travel memoir in 2004. He has also been featured in more than two dozen popular magazines including *Canadian Geographic, Backpacker, Explore, Canoe & Kayak,* and *BBC Wildlife.*

He currently lives with his wife Stacey in Vancouver, where they spend as much time hiking and kayaking as possible.